THAT
COLLEGE
BOOK

Everything *Nobody* Told Us About

Life After **High School**

by Timothy Snyder

THIS BLANK PAGE PUBLISHING

This Blank Page Publishing
Minneapolis, MN 55404
www.thisblankpage.com

Edited by: LuAnn Snyder, Kimberly Kelly
Cover Design: Timothy Snyder
Photography: Wil Galvez Photography

Snyder, Timothy
THAT COLLEGE BOOK: Everything Nobody Told Us About Life After High School / Timothy Snyder.
p. cm.
ISBN 978-1535243551

First Edition

4 8 1 5 1 6 2 3 4 2

Acknowledgements and Additional Notes

Before we begin, I'd just like to give a huge thanks to everyone who helped make this book possible. To those who have their story featured, thank you so much for sharing it with me, and then letting me share it in return. If I, by chance, forgot to get permission from you for sharing said story, I apologize. Please don't sue me.

I'd also like to specifically thank Wil Galvez for the beautiful photography he did for this project. The cover of this book and the website promoting it would be a lot uglier without you. Thanks to my mom for being my editor, not just with this book, but almost every important thing I've ever written. You are, without a doubt, the reason for my inner grammarist. Thanks to my dad for providing me with so many quotable moments you're about to read.

Thanks to my friends who have shown such patience with this whole thing as I've been talking about it for the past 5 years. It's finally here, so you better be reading it. And to those who read various rough drafts along the way, thanks for your efforts and your feedback. You have no idea how much you contributed to this end product.

Thank you, God, for giving me this untamable desire to write and create.

Lastly, a special mention to Alex Kubicek. If it wasn't for your enthusiastic response after reading an earlier draft on the cusp of your high school graduation, I honestly think I would have abandoned it altogether.

For those reading this now, I'm going to tell you that much of what you see here is not what would be considered "proper English". When it comes to writing, you learn as you grow older that as long as you know and respect the rules, you have free rein to break many of them. That said, it's not impossible that you might stumble upon an actual typo or two. If that happens, first of all, I'm sorry. Second, if you just want to shoot me an email about that, that'd be awesome. You can also track me down on social media. I tend to be under the handle *@thetimsnyder*.

And Jaron, since you didn't actually make it into the book, here is me mentioning your name. Congratulations.

- Timothy

Contents

Introduction:

The Road Unfortunately Taken

With each bump in the pavement, my rusting Ford Taurus shook violently. The mechanic said I needed new shocks and tie rods. I couldn't afford new shocks *or* tie rods. So I just had to deal with it.

Pressing hard on the gas, I watched as the orange needle on my dash went well over the speed limit. But speeding wasn't going to change my fate.

I was going to be late. I was going to be late for my college graduation rehearsal.

Why can't it be raining, I thought. If it were raining, I'd at least have some reason to give for being late. A horrific traffic accident might have worked too. Anything that was out of my control. Instead, the sky was cloudless, and the roads were clear.

Always late with little excuse; story of my life.

As I continued to push the limits of my rattling car, the ringtone on my phone sounded off beside me. I stole a glance from the screen. *Unknown caller*. I put my focus back on the road. I never answered calls from strangers. If it was important, they'd leave a message. That was my motto. Maybe it was just another failed excuse.

A few blocks later, and my message light started blinking. I had a voicemail. Now I was curious. Taking the steering wheel in my left hand, I reached for my little red LG phone. A couple of button presses, and I was listening to my mystery caller's message.

"Hey Timothy," said an unfamiliar male voice, "it's Panera Bread in Shakopee. I was just calling to let you know we received your application."

The caller just went from having my curiosity to having my full attention. I gripped the steering wheel tight in anticipation. Could my days of unemployment finally be at an end?

"You have great experience, and we would love to have you work with us."

I held my breath as I tried to remember what it was like to have regular income. After more than a year of odd jobs, rejected applications, and fragile finances, sweet, consistent paychecks were coming my way.

"Unfortunately..."

I felt my heart sink down into my stomach, dragging all my hopes and dreams down with it.

"...we just hired three new people and don't have any open positions. We usually have a new position open every couple of months. If something comes up, we'll let you know right away. Thanks Timothy. Once again, we'd love to have you. We just don't need anyone right now."

The phone fell from my hand, slipping into the abyss that lies between the driver's seat and the center console. I was 23 years old, driving to my college graduation rehearsal, a mere 5 days away from receiving a Bachelor's degree, and I just got rejected for an entry level position at Panera Bread.

Panera.

Freaking.

Bread.

I had applied to a job where 90% of my competition was high school students, and I lost. Most likely *to* high school students. Possibly middle-aged house wives. I guess it didn't matter that I had actual restaurant experience (not to mention, you know, a college degree). Like the phone that had just fallen from my hands, I felt as though I had been dropped out of life, slipping into some in-between space.

I no longer cared about being late to rehearsal. I wasn't concerned with how I was going to get my phone out of the crevice it fell into. I simply wondered how I ended up in this current predicament.

See, I grew up with this mental checklist of life: be born, go to school, graduate from school, go to college, graduate from college, start a career, get married, have a few kids, retire, die. In my understanding, that's just how life was, and if I followed that checklist line by line, I would win the game of life, achieve the American dream, find Waldo and all that jazz.

All I had to do was hit the checkpoints as they arose, like a linear round of Whack-a-Mole. They had started off so easy. It's not like I remember my birth. I suppose it would be pretty traumatic if anyone did. Thinking about it now, I completely understand why parents made up that whole "stork" thing. Regardless of how I was brought into this world, I saw my birth as the free-space on life's bingo card.

Next up was school. I never had a problem with school. On my first day of kindergarten, there was a boy in the corner crying. "I miss my mommy," he said between weeping gasps. Maybe school was hard for him, but for me, it was smooth sailing from day one. Oh sure, I went to the principal's office a few times, had my heart broken here and there, and the sixth grade as a whole was sort of awful, but besides that, I had lots of friends, I was involved in everything, and I made all sorts of memories.

And once I made it through high school, I got to experience step three: graduation.

Imagine all of your friends throwing parties at the exact same time. There is punch, cake, sandwiches, those shiny little confetti pieces, and you get money from people you don't even know. It kind of makes the whole school process worth it. Best of all, I was free. As I was handed my diploma, and stood there, a high school graduate, I realized the rest of my life was before me. It was time to choose a college which would lead to a career and all the other wonderful things on my life list. The problem was I had to choose.

3

Not whether or not I went to college. I *had to* go to college lest I become a jobless bum. At least, that's what I thought. So I had to decide where I would be going. Unfortunately, decision making isn't my strongest skill.

In a panic, I quickly chose a college and went. It was fun, exciting, and completely wrong for me. The next year, I would choose a different college and end up sticking with it. Four years later, I graduated with a Bachelor of Arts degree in English with an emphasis in creative writing.

Unfortunately, this is where my whole "life plan" train went completely off track, flipped on its side, crashed through a small town, and destroyed everything in its path. The only guarantee in life is that there are no guarantees in life. I hate clichés, but this one is particularly true. I knew what I wanted to be while I was in college, and I thought I had a job lined up that could lead me to that next step. Apparently, it didn't matter. I graduated jobless and flat broke with school loans knocking at my door like Death himself. I felt crippled, scared, and lost, not so different from my kindergarten classmate crying for his mommy.

All I could do was sit there and ask myself "How did I get here?"

That was back in 2010, and I can happily say that I am sitting in a much different position. You see, today I'm doing almost exactly what I planned on doing after college. My life is far from perfect, but I stand victorious-ish. I'm a college graduate with a career semi-relevant to what I went to college for, and I spend my free time chasing down the rest of my dreams and doing things that I love doing.

From what I understand, this is a bit of a rarity these days.

But despite my happier mood, better standing, and best efforts, I'm still paying for past missteps. Thanks to some poor choices, I racked up some serious debt. I also lost out on a good chunk of time I will never get back. The two years that followed my graduation were some of the darkest, most difficult years of my life. It's not just that they were challenging. I was completely lost, stuck in a hole with no visible way of getting out.

Life after college broke me, and to be transparent, I'm still working on reassembling the pieces.

In many ways, I feel like I should have been where I am now about 4-5 years ago. That's just how it is sometimes, and I've accepted that I can't change the past. But maybe I can help someone change their future. If I could survive and become the man I set out to be, surely someone could take what I've learned and do it better.

That's how the world advances. The future changes when you avoid the mistakes of the past.

When I graduated from college broke, jobless, and directionless, it wasn't because the economy was bad or because my parents weren't rich. I mean, sure, a better economy and rich parents wouldn't have hurt, but most of the blame lays on decisions that I made. It wasn't that I made one major wrong decision. The problem was that I made a series of poor, seemingly insignificant choices going back as far as high school that added up to disastrous results.

In a lot of cases, I made those decisions because I simply didn't know better. Often, I was just doing what I thought you were supposed to do.

I've spent a lot of time over the past few years talking with friends, family, and strangers who have experience all sorts of post-high school problems, and we kept coming back to the same questions:

Why didn't we know about THIS fact?

What made us think THAT would happen?

What if we would have gone THERE instead?

Why didn't someone tell me not to do THESE things?

Too many of us had bought into this idea that life is a one-way, single lane road where choice is an illusion, and everything will magically work itself out. We realized all too late that there were so many things that nobody told us about life after high school.

And I thought to myself *there should be a book about this.*

So, in an attempt to legitimize my English degree, I sat down to write one. Initially, it was a book about everything I wish that someone would have told *me* before I went and committed my life to this thing called college. While that's still the heart of the book, it has grown into something more. It's become the story of people who unexpectedly slipped into the gap between high school and adulthood, why it happened, and what might have prevented it.

A lot of people read books by famous people who have done famous things in a hope to mimic their actions and become famous themselves. This book is kind of the opposite. I'm not famous nor are any of the people featured here. Most of the stories you're about to read are ones of epic failure. Hopefully by reading them you can learn from them, avoid them, and become one of those super famous people who write how-to-succeed-in-life books. If that happens, I promise to read your book in return. Just make sure to thank me in the opening notes. Throw some royalties my way too, while you're at it.

Who is this book for? It's for people who are going to go to college, skipping college, or are in college right now. It's for people who know absolutely nothing about college and people who think they know everything about life after high school. It's for parents whose children may or may not go to college. It's for those who are searching and trying to figure out how they can get to that next point on the grand checklist of life.

And for people who have already been through college or have their career, feel free to read it anyway. This isn't a book of facts, figures, and statistics. It's a book of stories and experiences shared across a generation of people who were told to go to college *first*, and ask questions *later*.

I hope you learn something. I hope in some small way, it helps you make better decisions so that the struggles you face in life are better than the struggles I had to deal with the past few years. I also hope you find this book to be funny. That way, if it sucks, you can say "Well, that book was awful, but at least it made me smile."

Feel free to laugh at my personal pain. I do...when I'm not crying from it. If you're reading this book, and you aren't a personal friend or family member who had to read it out of obligation, then my trials and errors weren't for nothing. Hopefully this book didn't become a smashing success after I died a lonely, homeless death. I always felt sorry for authors who experienced that. I guess this book isn't for me though. It's for you, whoever you may be.

Enjoy. If you read something, and say to yourself, "Dang Tim, that stuff there is on point," feel free to tweet it, Facebook it, tumble it, tumble dry it, and whatever else you crazy kids do these days. Just throw #thatcollegebook at the end, and we're good to go.

Oh, and if I'm dead, shed a tear for me please.

Part I

To Go to College or Not to Go to College...

Is That Even a Question?

Chapter 1:

Don't Buy into the Hype

"College isn't for everyone.."

Ever notice how that's typically said in a negative context? It's as if they're really saying "Being successful isn't for everyone" or to be blunter, "Only really dumb, really poor, or really athletic people skip college." Does *not* going to college mean that you're some uneducated bum who's going to die in the same town they were born in?

Of course not.

Besides, almost everyone used to die in the same town they were birthed in, and they were great people. Granted, women used to smoke during pregnancy and baby cribs used to be painted with lead based paint, but the point I'm failing to make here is this: there is nothing wrong with not going to college.

I was raised with this idea that college was an inevitability. Like two plus two equaling four, high school graduation led to college attendance. It was never *if* I go to college. It was always *when* I go to college. I wish someone would have made it clear that college was my choice, and that a good life could still be had without stepping foot into a college classroom.

People can have great success without going to college. No, I'm not talking about rockstars or actors. I'm talking about normal people in normal jobs. People who *chose* not to go to college.

11

If you're going to go that route though, you're going to have to be committed. You're going to have to work hard. You're going to have to know what you want to do and where you want to be.

In other words, you have to have a plan.

Joey's Story

Joey is a former roommate of mine. He's also a ginger. Not that it matters. I just want to help you get a visualization. Despite being 2.5 years younger than me and not having any college education, Joey is arguably more successful than myself. Why doesn't he write a book then? Well, writing isn't Joey's strong suit. But what he lacks in rhetorical skills, he makes up for with a dedicated work ethic.

Back in high school, Joey wanted a job so he could make some spending money. See, Joey needed to impress the ladies, and girls don't like broke, jobless boys unless they're musicians. Joey was not a musician. So, he started working at a popular restaurant chain. The occupation was nothing fancy, but Joey discovered he was pretty good at it. Soon, he found himself promoted.

As high school graduation approached, Joey considered the college route. The idea seemed attractive. All of his friends were heading to college. There were plenty of fun times to be had. The problem was, Joey had no idea what he would get a degree in. Truth was, he had never cared much for school. Meanwhile, his job offered him the promise of future promotions. After graduating, Joey took a leap of faith and decided to work full time at his current job.

Four years after starting that job, Joey became a General Manager of his own store. He was 22 at the time. The job came with salary pay, paid vacation, the ability to write his own schedule, and quite a bit of free food. Oh, and he had zero college debt. Instead of spending hours learning about subjects he didn't care about, Joey learned how to build a team, manage inventory, delegate finances, and make a wide variety of food and beverage items. I can tell you first hand that he enjoys his job and takes pride in what he does. And he still has room for further promotion, should he choose to go that route.

By comparison, when I was 22 years old, I was still in college, racking up the last few thousand dollars of my debt. I did have a job at the time. Sort of. It was for a commercial moving company. The available hours were all over the place, and I got paid $10 an hour. Most of the time, we'd go in at 6am and move really heavy things. I did not enjoy it. I did not take pride in it. And there was no road for advancement. I made just enough to cover my rent. Meanwhile, Joey was making a living for himself.

That's not to say it's all about money and job security. This wouldn't be a success story if deep down, Joey hated his job. But he doesn't. Overall, he's enjoyed it very much. Will it be what he does for the rest of his life? Only time will tell. I do know that, should he decide to pursue something else, his manager experience can help greatly in landing him a job elsewhere.

Despite what I thought for a long time, there are still plenty of "real jobs" out there that can be attained without a college degree. They're not some made up fantasy like the Easter Bunny or fat-free pizza. They exist. You just need to find them and work hard to earn them. It's also important that you actually *want* to do them. Like Joey's own position, many of these jobs start off as part time or entry level. A lot of companies promote from within, meaning almost everyone has to start at the ground level regardless of education or experience.

I've worked a lot of jobs in my day, and with each one of them, I never stopped to think of where they might lead. I never thought how I'd feel if I was still working there 3 or 4 years from now. All I cared about was making some money to hold me over.

It might seem weird to think about when you're looking for a part time job, but it never hurts to consider advancement potential when you're applying somewhere. While considering a job, ask yourself this: If you're still working there three or four years from now, will you have a better position? Will you be making more money? Will you still find a sense of purpose or fulfillment in your work?

These are all questions you might want to seriously consider.

The Safe Start

Community college: it's where you go if you're too dumb to get into a real school, right?

Wrong.

Okay, sure, some people do go to community college to bring up their poor grades, but many choose to go there for a variety of other reasons. If you want a four-year degree, a masters, or a doctorate, are you going to get it at a community college? Generally, no. But you can still start there. As you probably know, there are certain college classes that everyone has to take (yes, unfortunately mathematics is one of them). Community college might be just the place to get these classes out of the way while you figure out what you want to do with your life.

Depending on where you end up going to college, taking some general classes at a community college could save you quite a bit of money. Think of it like Nyquil cold medicine vs. the store-brand variant. Nyquil might be a little more effective, but at the end of the day, both will knock you unconscious, allowing you to sleep without sneezing and coughing. The difference is, Nyquil is about $2 more per bottle.

If you want to go to a four-year school eventually but you're looking to save yourself some money, there is absolutely nothing wrong with looking into community college as a place to start.

In fact, you can take community college classes while you're enrolled at another college or university. Sadly, no one told me this until my last semester of college. It was spring 2010. Sunrays danced along sparse, white clouds in the sky. A cool breeze pushed against my overly-spiked hair, making me look like the male lead of a Japanese anime. I had just crossed 12th St in Minneapolis when I saw my friend Corey getting into his car.

"Hey Corey," I said, "Where are you off to?"

"Oh, I got Spanish down at Normandale," said Corey.

"You're not a student here anymore?" I asked, quite surprised.

"No, I am."

"But...Normandale."

"Yeah," he said as if I just said something really stupid, "That's where I'm taking Spanish."

"You're taking college within college?"

"I guess."

"That's legal?"

"Yep."

"Why?"

"Why is it legal?"

"No, why are you taking it there?"

"Because their Spanish class is $1000 cheaper."

"Why does no one tell me these things!?" I shouted as I ran away in shame.

This news probably would have hurt a little less had I not been currently enrolled in our school's more expensive Spanish class. I didn't even like Spanish. Had I known I could take college classes outside of my school while remaining enrolled in that school, I probably would have taken a different language altogether. I would have saved $1000 and been well on my way to learning Japanese. Japanese, I say! The people in that class would have appreciated my hair so much.

It wasn't really until that happened that I realized there might be more to the community college scene than I ever gave it credit for. Maybe I should have been a little more like my brother and sister.

A Tale of Two Siblings

In the town of Sheldon, Iowa, there is a lovely little community college called NCC. I know this because this is where I grew up. Sheldon is pretty small (i.e. 5000 people) and doesn't have much in it. To better paint the picture, we just got a McDonalds a couple of years ago, and it was a big deal. Yet, despite being barely populated farm country, Sheldon has a community college. Why? Because like rain in Seattle or hipsters in Minneapolis, Minnesota, community colleges are everywhere.

Availability is one of the reasons why community colleges are so convenient, and convenience is the exact reason why my brother and sister both attended NCC.

Being the oldest of us siblings, my brother was the first to head off to college. It was a pretty big deal. The first baby bird leaving the nest. Only he didn't really leave. Upon graduating from high school, my brother Tony signed up for classes at NCC. It wasn't his endgame strategy, but for the moment it made a lot of sense. His classes would be incredibly cheap, the school was practically in our backyard, and he could keep his current job whilst freeloading off of our parents.

"Are you glad you went to community college?" I asked my brother as I secretly planned to use his response in this book.

"Yeah, I guess so," he responded. That was the end of the conversation.

My brother: a man of few words. Allow me to elaborate for him. He has nothing to regret about going to community college for a year. He saved money while figuring out where he wanted to go, and what he wanted to do with his life. When he left for a four-year college the next year, he seemed quite sure that was the right decision.

In fact, it worked out so well for him that my older sister followed in his footsteps the following year. Her story is almost the exact same. After a year of community college, she ended up going to the same college as my brother. It was there that she earned her degree *and* met her husband.

What a happy ending, huh? Had she been afraid of going to community college, who knows where she would have ended up?

Probably living in a van down by the Floyd River in Sheldon, Iowa.

So why didn't I go to community college like my brother and sister? For a long time, I said it was because it simply wasn't the right choice for me. Truth is, I didn't want to be one of those people who stayed around after college. I wanted to venture out and start a new life. In this case, I think that worked out just fine. When it comes to big life decisions, there isn't always a *right* and *wrong* choice.

Then again, sometimes there is.

The Point of No Return

The summer air was thick with humidity as black clouds began to swell and blanket the sky. Thunder crackled, declaring that rain was coming. As the first few droplets pattered against the windshield of the Volkswagen Jetta I sat inside of, I quickly rolled my window up. Though I was protected from the inevitable downpour, a different storm was brewing inside the car. In the driver's seat next to me sat my friend Rachel.

Even with the sun lost in darkness behind the clouds above, it wasn't hard to see the tears forming in her eyes.

The rain was now beating away against the aluminum roof, demanding that its presence be known. The change in moisture caused the windows to fog over, leaving us nearly blind to the maelstrom outside. We weren't going anywhere anytime soon. Rachel turned her head away from me, but I could see the confusion in the edges of her face.

"I just wish I could go back," she said.

My heart sank. That's exactly how I had felt the past year. Longing to return to a simpler time where I could change my poor decisions. It was a desire that had wreaked havoc over my mind. I couldn't go back. I couldn't reverse time and unmake my choices. And this was the pain in

Rachel's voice. You see, Rachel is one of the most responsible people I know. Like most things in her life, she had her future all planned out. As her high school graduation approached, she was set on going to a community college called Normandale. It was close, it was cheap, and it would provide all of the classes she needed for now. Unfortunately, not everyone felt the same.

Rachel had a teacher whose opinion was very important to her. This teacher strongly urged her to go to a "real school", saying that community college would hold her back. Right before she committed to going to Normandale, she changed her mind and applied for a university instead. Being a respectable student, she was accepted in no time. In the moment, it seemed like a good choice to go to this university. Three years later, it was obvious that it had been the wrong choice.

"I knew it wasn't right," she said while we were stuck in the car. "I knew it then just like I know it now. I should have gone to Normandale. There was nothing stopping me. I made the wrong decision."

Rachel's teacher had great intentions. He saw a lot of potential in Rachel and wanted the best for her. The problem was, the best thing for Rachel just might have been community college. Attending Normandale for a few semesters wouldn't have decreased her future options whatsoever. Having three-fourths of a degree at a private university practically extinguished them. Instead of being empowered by her education, Rachel became burdened by it.

Having that much of a degree completed at one specific private school is very hard to transfer. As for leaving it unfinished, that's a waste of a lot of money. On a résumé, an unfinished degree isn't much different from no degree at all.

On that night when Rachel and I were stuck in her car, I wanted to tell her that everything was going to be okay. I wanted to remind her of the awesome person she was. But what Rachel really needed at that moment was to simply let it all out. To admit that she had made a mistake.

Had she done it sooner, there might have been more options available than simply soldiering on.

There will come points in your life where you have to make hard decisions. In those times, there will be people around you whom you love and respect that will give you their opinion. Some of them will be nice and subtle about it. Others will be very blunt and brash. All of them will mean well.

But that doesn't mean they'll be right.

They could be. It's possible that they're seeing something you are blinded to because you're too close to the situation or because you lack confidence in yourself. They could also be completely wrong because they're not you. They don't carry your calling. They can't experience the things you feel deep down inside.

When those moments come, if you know without question what the right choice is, you have to have the courage to make the call. After all, you're the one who has to bear the consequences.

Community Colleges are Like Dogs (In a Good Way)

I'm friends with this married couple. Actually, I'm friends with a lot of married couples. You reach this point in your life when at least three-fourths of your friends are engaged or married. Depending on your romantic life, you'll either be really excited or a bit depressed.

Possibly both at the same time.

Anyway, the particular couple I'm talking about are my friends Roy and Elissa. Like many loving married couples, they had dreams of a family filled with little children running around. Being quite young and new to the world of careers, mortgages, and bills upon bills, they knew that the first years of their marriage weren't a time for children. But that desire to raise and care for something remained. So what did they do?

They bought a dog.

Their dog was named River and she was a black, lion-sized creature who enjoyed tackling people and chewing on their feet. What I'm saying is River was quite a handful that required Roy and Elissa to be more responsible. Still, as crazy as she was, River was not a baby. Compared to babies, dogs are much cheaper, easier to train, and sometimes, it's perfectly okay to tie them up outside and ignore them for a bit. That doesn't really fly with babies. Roy and Elissa knew they ultimately wanted to have a baby, but they were smart enough to realize they weren't ready.

So instead, they took a small step that helped prepare them for the ultimate goal ahead.

Just so we're clear, I'm not saying you should run out and adopt a puppy or make a baby. I'm saying that college is a big step that takes considerable time and commitment and not everyone is ready for that straight out of high school. If you know you want to go to college, but you're not sure if you're ready, community college might be the perfect solution for you. Decisions can't be unmade, but sometimes, you can delay them for a little bit.

If you're ready for the full college experience, go for it. If you're not, take it slow.

For so much of my life, I was told to take things slow. Whether I was behind the wheel or pursuing a pretty girl, 'taking it slow' was generally advised as the best course of action. But when it came to college, for whatever reason, that changed, and I was basically told to jump in head first and learn how to swim after. So just in case you've received similar advice, I'm here to say there is nothing wrong with taking it slow.

Pretend you're a gentleman from the 1800s and college is a classy lady. Court her. Meet her parents. Weigh the pros and cons of your arrangement with her. And when the time is right, the stars align, and everything is agreed upon, take her hand in holy matrimony.

Or something like that...

Where's the Cake?

For the past few decades, there has been an idea placed in the minds of almost every high school student. It's as if we've all been incepted. The idea is that if you work hard and go through college, you will be rewarded with a plethora of jobs to choose from once you graduate. Many of my friends and I went to college thinking that once it ended, there was to be a grand party that acts as a kick start to our adult lives. This party will have all of our friends and family cheering us on, and sitting on a table is a great big cake with our names written on it.

Let me break this to you: the cake is a lie.

Stop me if you've heard this one. "If you go to college, you will get a great paying job upon graduating that you will take great pride in." I've heard teachers say that. I've heard parents say that. I think I've even heard a president or two say it. This is a more accurate version of that statement: "If you go to college, you *might* get a *decent* paying job upon graduating that you're not completely embarrassed by. Oh, and you'll only get that after sending out endless résumés and cover letters. You might need an internship or two as well."

Doesn't sound as sexy, does it?

Sure, some people get lucky when they graduate. They have great connections or rich uncles who made a fortune in the wild-west days of the internet, and they get a nice, cush job right out of the gates. But for so many college graduates, after years of working their butt off in classes to make the grade, they have to work their butt off just to get a passable job. Post-grad life is a big game, and the game tends to be both rigged and not a lot of fun. Be prepared. Oh, and that party I mentioned earlier. That doesn't happen either.

A couple years ago, my good friend Alex graduated from college. He needed a new place to live, and I had a spare bedroom waiting to be filled so he moved in the day of his graduation. I had been gone that weekend, leaving Alex and his parents access to the house in my absence. I returned a few days later to find Alex sitting alone in his new bedroom.

"What's up, broseph?" I asked, completely forgetting that I told myself I would stop using the word *broseph*.

"Nothing actually," he said. "Absolutely nothing."

"Oh," I paused, looking over the mostly unpacked room. "All moved in?"

"Yep. Didn't really have much."

"Parents gone?"

"Yeah, they left right after moving me in."

I smirked. "Let me guess, you had your graduation ceremony, went out to dinner, parents moved you in, left, and you sat here by yourself for the last couple days, feeling lonely and wondering what the crap you're doing with your life."

Alex nodded. "How'd you know?"

"That's exactly how my graduation went."

"Well, you're right. I've been sitting in here like an idiot. Everyone was either busy or gone."

"Welcome to post-college life. It's not all they say it is."

"Yeah man," he said, "it actually kind of sucks."

Quick question: which is featured more often in movies? High school graduation or college graduation? The answer is high school graduation. Do you know why that is? It's because high school graduations are considerably more exciting than college graduations. College ceremonies are longer, less familiar, and there's a good chance you won't be graduating with your friends. Once it's over, your diploma is shipped out, and you're left to fend for yourself.

When I graduated from college, I went to my ceremony, ate dinner with my parents, and then they took off. There was no big after-party. I received one congratulatory letter. When my degree came in the mail, I set it up on my dresser where it proceeded to collect dust like a champ. Even a year or two afterwards, I would have people ask when I was going to graduate from college. Was I supposed to send announcements out to everyone? I'm sorry, I was too busy not getting a job.

I apologize if I'm sounding bitter or depressing. It's not my intention. I just want to be straight with you; college graduations tend to be underwhelming. If you're saying to yourself, "I'm going to go to college because when I graduate, everything is going to be perfect and fantastical as I ride across dream-filled rainbows on my fire-breathing unicorn named Cornelius", you're setting yourself up for disappointment.

I think this best describes it:

Growing up, my life was an island. Everything I knew, everything I was, was on the island. When high school graduation came, it was like moving from inland out to the beach of my island. The beach was awesome and the horizon seemed to stretch on forever.

I'd sit there, and I'd think *I wonder what's beyond this island?*

Then college graduation came, and that was like moving from the beach out into the middle of the ocean. Suddenly, life was sink or swim. I couldn't just go back to the island that I knew. I couldn't even see the shore. Some days, I questioned if there was ever an island in the first place.

Meanwhile, sharks were circling, ready to devour me. It felt as if I could be swallowed up at any moment, disappearing into the watery abyss forever.

That is exactly the scenario I would like to help people avoid. It's why I am writing this book in the first place. No one wants to be lost at sea. No one wants to feel like life moved on without them. And while you could argue that this type of situation is inevitable in life, it at least deserves to be caused by something grander than just "finishing college".

The Boy that God Forgot About

Facebook is a great place to keep in touch with friends and family. It's not a great place for serious conversations. That doesn't mean they don't still happen. I was sitting comfortably on my roommate's suede couch, laptop in front me when a chat window popped up. It was my friend Chris. Things started off light and breezy. He asked how I was. I lied and said everything was great. This was during the two-year post-college darkness period. I didn't want to get too serious on the Facebook, so I decided not to mention that my life felt meaningless. Chris, on the other hand, had other plans in mind....

Chris: Tim, can I ask you a serious question?

Timothy: Sure.

Chris: I'm warning you, it's a big one.

Timothy: Is it about the deeper themes and ideas of the Battlestar Galactica finale?

Chris: No, it's about the deeper themes and ideas of my life.

Timothy: Oh...

Chris: Yeah.

Timothy: Well, now I'm a little nervous, but we're standing too close to not dance at this point.

Chris: K. I know it sounds juvenile at best, but...why do I feel like God forgot about me?

Timothy: You're asking why you feel like God forgot about you?

Chris: Precisely! I feel like He straight up forgot about me.

Timothy: Could you maybe elaborate a little bit?

And elaborate he did. This isn't a conversation of faith or whether you believe there is a God. It's about feeling lost. Cheated, even. My friend Chris worked hard in college. He studied, held a job, poured himself into an internship, and produced a very solid senior project. Basically, he did everything right. Surely everything would come together after graduation, right?

Not so much.

Since he was living in an on-campus apartment, he had to move out soon after graduation. His part time job's hours weren't ideal and the work environment was becoming increasingly less fulfilling. As for the internship, the hope that it would turn into a permanent position was quickly diminishing. In the span of a month, years of plans came undone and Chris's world had become completely foreign to him. To make things worse, most of his college friends were slipping away, leaving him with few people to confide in. Oh, and he went through a rather serious breakup right in the middle of it all.

"I feel like I'm living an edited life. Some short, undeveloped outline of what it should have been," Chris had said to me.

Much like myself, Chris had lived his college days with a certain amount of blind optimism, the idea that everything would fall into place like a rigged game of connect four. Then reality happened. The blinders were removed and for the first time, Chris glimpsed life's raw, unfinished center.

Handling the Truth

For both Chris and myself (and many others), post-college living was the first time the bumpers were taken off life's bowling lane. We weren't going into graduate studies, leaving us without an automatic next step. We no longer had our parents to provide for us or teachers to teach us.

It wasn't until I graduated from college that I realized how much control I had over my life, and ironically, it left me feeling incredibly helpless.

Put simply, the post college transition can be the hardest, and most painful season of life that a young person has ever faced up to that point. It doesn't relent. Author Phillip K. Dick once said "Reality is that which, when you stop believing in it, doesn't go away." I spent most of college (and even some of high school) putting off reality as much as possible. For a while, I had myself convinced that I had succeeded. But all I had done was delay the inevitable. The longer you put off the realities of life, the harder they will hit you. So what do you do?

You accept them and step towards something greater.

Like metal is forged in fire, between an anvil and a hammer, the struggles of your early adulthood will shape you into the person you will be for the rest of your life. The sooner you accept your responsibilities, the less painful it's going to be. Moving on from college and starting my real life has been exciting. It's been an adventure filled with all sorts of twists and turns. But so much of it felt like I was playing catch-up. Generally, it's better to form a battle plan before the battle. That would be the smart thing to do, anyway.

Chapter 2:

Don't be Stupid

Imagine that you're going to buy a car.

You spend weeks scrolling through websites and visiting dealerships, hoping to find something you can be proud of. After what feels like an eternity, you find her: the car of your dreams. She's red and shiny with chrome rims, dual exhaust, and a moonroof! Just standing beside her makes you weak in the knees, and when the salesman revs the engine for you, it makes the hairs on your neck stand up.

After you stop drooling long enough to form a sentence, you tell Mr. Salesman that this is the car you've been searching for your entire life. He says something about "the driver don't pick the car, the car picks the driver," which doesn't make a lot of sense to you. But you don't care.

You just want this car.

He brings you into an office where you fill out an encyclopedia of paperwork, signing your name so many times, you feel like a celebrity. Finally, the salesman puts the paperwork away and hands you the keys. The car is yours! Congratulations. You are now legally and financially bound to this vehicle. There's just one problem:

You have no idea how to drive a car.

Sure, you understand the basic concepts. There are pedals on the floor. One makes the car go, the other makes it stop. Also, there are these levers and a big wheel in front of the driver's seat that's really fun to turn back and forth. As if that wasn't enough to soak in, there's more confusion to owning a car! You aren't entirely sure how you're going to make payments on it, and you really don't understand this whole "car insurance" concept. And what happens if something breaks?

But hey, you have a car! That's all that matters. Everything is going to be fine because you have a car.

This story makes absolutely no sense, right? Why would anyone buy a car when they don't know how to drive? You'd have to be a complete idiot to do that. And yet, if you replace the car with college, there are hundreds of thousands of students who do this exact thing every year. I know this because I was one of them.

My name is Timothy Snyder, and I am a recovering idiot.

When I was nearing the end of high school, I understood the basic idea of college. I had heard teachers talk about it all the time. I had two siblings who were in college. My parents had even gone to college.

I knew that I could pick a major which would affect what classes I took. I knew there was a "campus" that had rooms called "dorms" where I would live. My dad made sure to inform me that because my grades weren't perfect, and I didn't work enough, I would have to take out these things called "loans" as well. At the age of 18, loans were an entirely different mystery in and of themselves.

But despite all my ignorance, I took off straight for college anyway, committing myself to something I didn't even understand. And like I said earlier, I'm not the only one who has done this.

The Worst College Student Ever

Once upon a time, there lived a Midwestern boy named Ryan. Ryan lived in a small town with his mom, his dad, two brothers, a sister, and their little dog. While Ryan was a likable guy, he wasn't exactly the most motivated human being. Most of his nights and weekends consisted of finding the biggest, craziest parties. In between his misadventures, he found time to do just enough school work to graduate on time. Ryan didn't like school at all, but he was very keen on graduating.

Like so many Midwestern youth, Ryan was eager to escape his small-town residency. College seemed like the perfect opportunity to do so.

Ryan had decided he was going to a magical kingdom called Valley City State University. What made him decide on this school? The answer is quite simple. They were the first ones to mail him information. Not that he actually read that information. No, Ryan simply looked at a few pictures and decided that it would do. Many colleges will accept just about anyone with a high school diploma, and Ryan was accepted shortly after sending in his application.

He had a ticket out of his hometown, VCSU had a new student, and everyone was happy! Unfortunately for Ryan, this was just the setup for a tragic story.

Since Ryan didn't work much and his grades weren't exactly scholarship material, he took out loans to pay for all of his school expenses. He was amazed at how easy the loans were to attain. It was as if he were receiving free money. Who's going to turn down free money? Dumb people, that's who!

There were a lot of things Ryan didn't understand that first year of college. Things like choosing classes or deciding on a major. Instead, he just decided to take what sounded cool. It didn't really matter because Ryan never went to class. You see, without his parents and teachers watching over him, Ryan's easy going attitude mutated into a complete lack of care and concern for his life. The bad habits he developed in high school exploded like a flame exposed to pure oxygen.

Ryan's life was on the verge of going supernova.

One semester in, and Ryan had only passed one of his classes. He was also getting close to being kicked out of his dorm because, well, he wasn't doing nice things. Rather than get kicked out or change his ways, he decided to move into an apartment (which was against school policy).

Since Ryan wasn't officially out of his dorm, he was paying rent for two places at once. Now that he had absolutely no rules to live under, Ryan went to complete rock-star status, partying every night until he passed out, never remembering exactly what had happened when he woke up the next day.

Finally, a week before his second semester finals, he decided to drop out of college altogether. In one year of college, Ryan racked up $18,000 of debt, received three minors for drinking, lost his driver's license, and only had three college credits to show for it.

With all other options exhausted, Ryan was forced to move back into his parents' house, living in the hometown he so desperately tried to get away from. And this time around, he couldn't drive and was flat broke. Thankfully, this isn't the end of Ryan's story.

But we'll get to the rest later.

The Breakdown

It's possible that you fully understand how the college system works. Congrats. You're smarter than Ryan and I were at the age of 18. Why don't you just skip this chapter and go hang out with your cool, smart friends? Or maybe you don't need to worry about college loans because of scholarships or because your parents are paying your way. If that's the case, I want you to realize how fortunate you are. You should also understand that a part of me dislikes you for that. Don't worry, I'm sure we can still be friends.

For the rest of us everyday people, allow me to fill you in on some concepts you may not fully grasp.

One thing I didn't understand until halfway through my sophomore year was credit hours. I'm not proud of this fact. It's quite embarrassing. People always talked about how much college cost per year. That left me with this impression that everyone paid the same amount each semester, taking however many classes they desired to. Maybe you think that's how it works too. Maybe you like to eat chalk and pretend it's candy. We all have our flaws.

Truth is, there are some colleges that work that way. More so now than when I was starting college. But that's not how mine worked. Please bear with me as I talk about some boring number stuff. I just want to make sure we're all on the same page here (like I said, if you know it, or you're absolutely never going to college, feel free to skip ahead).

Many colleges charge you per credit. Different classes are worth different amounts of credits. For example, a math class may be worth four credits while PE classes are typically one credit. Let's say your college charges you $500 per credit (which mine did). That means your math class will cost you $2000 while your PE class will cost you $500.

Is it a little scary that a math class can cost twice as much as my first car? Yes, it absolutely is. In this system of schooling, the more credits you take per semester, the more money you are going to pay out that year. If you want to be considered a full-time student, you'll need to take at least 12 credits. Typically, the maximum amount of credits you can take in a semester is 18 (though there are ways around that). If you want to maximize your financial aid or delay your current loans without being penalized, you'll need to be a full time student.

Of course, credit hours aren't the only thing you pay for at college. There are enrollment fees, housing fees, meal plans, lab fees, technology fees, and sometimes, you'll even get charged for something called a "miscellaneous fee". Apparently, your school needed just a little bit more money from you because *"reasons"*. Oh, and don't forget about your textbooks. As you may know, those are not provided to you in college. You must purchase them yourself.

Remember how your high school teacher used to say that the Exploring English Literature textbook you were so eager to set on fire cost over $100? Remember how you and your classmates thought that teacher was lying? They weren't. I've heard of textbooks that cost $200 or more.

Just imagine dropping $500+ on books for one semester. Books you don't even really want to read.

It's frightening. Like, blood-in-the-stool frightening.

The good news is you can sell them once your class is over. The bad news is you'll generally get about a tenth of what you paid for them. I've seen grown men tear up as they sold their $120 book for $17.83.

But as sad as all of that is, it's not as sad as the fact that I didn't know any of that when I started college. Not credit costs or fees or textbooks or full-time vs. part-time. Nothing. And because of that, I skipped out on a pretty-big opportunity.

What if You Could Have It All for Free!?

Back when I was in high school, once a student had all their required classes taken care of, they could start taking college classes. It seemed pretty cool at the time. You got to leave school, drive out to the local community college, maybe grab some Taco Johns, and feel like a college student for an hour or two. I found the concept so appealing that I took two college courses my senior year.

Western Civilization 1 and Western Civilization 2.

There were two specific things I did not grasp about this situation. First, taking Western Civ 1 saved me about $1500-$2000 in the long run. Second, most college degrees require only one semester of history, which means taking Western Civ 2 was completely unnecessary. Thank you to my high school guidance counselor for *not* pointing that out to me.

Now this whole process has different names depending on what state you live in. It's possible that your state doesn't offer it. If that's the case, you should call your local senator. If they won't take your calls, write them a very stern letter. These sorts of programs can save you some serious money and help you figure out what you want to do with your life! All before you even graduate from high school.

Here's how it works: You go to college and takes classes like any other student. Meanwhile, your school pays the bill, including the textbook! In other words, you get college *for free!*

To this day, I view this as one of my most wasted opportunities in life.

An Embarrassing Conversation

"High school is so dumb," said the girl standing before me. "I can't wait till next year."

"Why? You still have two years left," I said.

"Not really," the girl said.

"Are you dropping out?"

"No. Why would I do that? That would be stupid. Do you think I'm stupid?"

"Well...no. I just thought you, uh, might be pregnant?"

"Do I look pregnant?"

"It could be your first trimester."

"I'm going to pretend you didn't just say that."

"That makes two of us. So why are you so excited for next year?"

"Because I'll be taking all college classes."

"Okay, now I'm totally lost."

"Well, I still have a couple classes to take at high school like PE. Gross. But most of my classes will be at college."

"But you'll be a junior next year."

"Yep."

"And you'll be taking almost all college classes?"

"Yeah. Are you even listening?"

"So by the time you actually graduate and go off to college, you'll practically be a junior in *college*?"

"Pretty much."

"Why....why didn't I do this?"

"Well Tim," she said as her 5-foot frame suddenly seemed to tower over me, "Guess you're just not as smart as I am."

And then she walked away, leaving me alone with my embarrassment. No one likes to get burned by a 16-year-old girl. Especially college guys. Suddenly, the high school classes I took just for fun, those years of band and choir, they all seemed so insignificant.

Just like this student, I had the opportunity to complete a good chunk of college by the time I graduated from high school. I could have saved tens of thousands of dollars. My monthly loan bills would be considerably smaller.

Instead, I took two semesters of Western Civilization.

Seriously Though, What are You Waiting For?

If you're in high school, and you know you will be attending college sooner or later, why not get ahead of the game? Imagine if someone gave you advanced screening tickets for a movie you desperately wanted to see. Would you throw away those tickets so that you could go to concert band practice? Doubtful.

I'm not saying you shouldn't be involved in high school. Some of my fondest memories are from the different teams, productions, and organizations I was a part of in high school. But there comes a point where priorities need to be placed. Personally, I would have had no problem not being in band or choir my last semester of high school. The spring was always pretty boring anyway, and in place of those two groups, I could have probably taken at least two more college courses.

Which could have saved me around $4000.

Take a moment to think of just how much money $4000 is. When you're dealing with the tens of thousands of dollars that college costs, it's easy to trivialize these "smaller" amounts. But $4000 isn't small. If you're still in high school, that might be more than you make in a year. For me, that's about 10 months' worth of rent. If someone handed me $4000 right now, I would hug that person. I might even start crying a little bit.

And I'm not a crier. Not at all.

You might not want to, but there comes a moment in life when you need to weigh your current choices against the future results. Ten years from now, what is going to mean more to you? That last semester of chess club? Or finishing a four-credit college-class for free? I think that even as an 18-year-old kid who didn't understand the cost of college, I would have taken another college course or two if someone had strongly advised me to do so.

And if I had done so, I could have gotten math out of the way.

As I mentioned earlier, every four-year degree has certain general classes that everyone must take. These include but are not limited to math, science, English, history, and depending on whether you want a Bachelor of Arts or a Bachelor of Science, a foreign language class. By the time I got around to taking math in college, it had been over three years since I had taken a math class. By then, I didn't remember much past basic division. I ended up getting through just fine, but the journey was about as pleasant as a colonoscopy without anesthesia. I had a friend who failed college math twice. I bet he wishes he would have just gotten it out of the way in high school too.

Now, some people reading this may still be unsure about this whole college experience. The beautiful thing about college classes, particularly general classes like math and English, is that they can be saved and transferred to different schools later on. Once a class is taken, it becomes a part of your official transcript. Your transcript is a list of all the college classes you have ever been a part of as well as the grades you received in those classes.

Due to my transferring of colleges, my transcript is ridiculously long. I often use my excessive amount of credits to try and impress the ladies. It doesn't really work. And to think, I paid for all but eight of those credits.

Anyway, if there's a strong chance you'll be attending college at some point, and you have the chance to take some free courses, I would go ahead and do it.

A side note. College courses can technically expire. A lot of it depends on what the class was and where you're trying to transfer it to. I just wanted to mention that so that 30 years from now, you don't come track me down and say "Hey Tim, why won't Harvard accept my biology class I took in high school?"

And I would say "Well, our understanding of biology in the past 30 years has changed entirely. Everything you learned is completely outdated. Maybe you shouldn't have taken so long to go back to school."

Then you'll cry, and I'll stand there awkwardly. It won't be much fun for either of us.

Don't Say I Didn't Warn You

College is not cheap. Saying that is like saying excessive amounts of fast food will make you obese and give you heart trouble; it shouldn't really need to be said, and yet, people don't seem to fully grasp the concept. I sure didn't. Until I started paying for it, that is. At one point, my school debt was consuming about half of my monthly income. HALF!

And you thought the government took a lot of your money.

What's worse is that college is continually getting more expensive. My dad used to be a carpenter, which meant I often played the role as carpenter's assistant growing up. Even though he's "retired" from that line of duty, he still finds himself fixing things now and again. The last summer I spent at home during college, my dad and I were up on a roof. The sun was radiating off the tar of the shingles, raising the temperature by a good 15-20 degrees. My hands were dirtied and blistering. My feet were tired. This is what my dad considers "quality" father and son bonding time.

"You better get used to working," my dad said. "You'll be paying those college bills pretty soon like your brother and sister."

"Thanks for reminding me, dad," I said as I lifted a massive pile of old shingles and threw them into the truck below.

"Well you know, I made my last college payment the week before graduation," my dad said.

"Yes, dad, I know," I responded, now collecting the shingles with extra aggression. "You tell me this every year."

"And my parents didn't help me at all."

"Well that sounds familiar..." I said softly as I threw another load off the roof.

"What was that?" my dad asked.

"I said, uh, how much did a credit hour cost then?"

My dad stood up and wiped the sweat off his sunburnt brow with a gloved hand. "Let's see, at one point I was paying about 12 or 13 dollars per credit."

I stopped still. "Are you serious?"

"Yes. What are you paying?"

"$500 a credit!"

"Well, prices sure have gone up. You can thank the government for that."

"But we went to the same school. When did you go there? The 1850's?"

"Funny," my dad replied as he got back to work.

Pulling my phone out of my pocket, I quickly opened the calculator app. After a few button presses, my jaw dropped in horror.

"I paid 40 times more than you did?" I yelled. "40 times! Are you kidding me?"

"Should have gotten more scholarships," he replied. That was my dad. Ever the voice of reason and truth.

I'm not saying it would have been impossible for me to work my way through college, but I think it would have been a lot harder for me than it was for my dad. So, rather than paying for school outright, I took out these lovely little things called loans. Getting a loan is sort of like getting a puppy....if at the age of four, that puppy turned into a demonic presence that consumed your happiness.

A Rude Awakening

I knew loans were something not to be taken lightly. At least, I remembered being told that once or twice. But it seemed like college loans were different, like they were better or more socially acceptable. After all, my brother and sister took out college loans. Most of my friends were taking out college loans. Wanting to fit in with all the cool kids, I started taking out college loans too. In my defense, I didn't really have much of a choice. Financial aid only covered so much. I could only work so many hours. Truthfully, I thought I had a handle on the whole loan business.

I thought that for about 5 years. Then the bills started coming, and I realized somewhere along the way, I lost control of the situation entirely.

When I was a freshman in college, I took out a loan from the Bank of North Dakota (because that's where my college was). It didn't seem like too much at the time. Since my parents had three kids in college and weren't rich, I received a solid amount of financial aid (including this beautiful thing called a Pell Grant). Mapping out the next four or five years in my head, it appeared that I would have a manageable amount of money to pay back at the end of college.

But with my Sophomore year, a snowball effect started.

As I've mentioned, I transferred colleges after my freshman year. My second college was a little more expensive, but nothing too drastic. However, my brother was now independent from my parents, leaving them with only two kids in college. Also, they were both making more money. These two factors took a surprising toll on my financial aid, stripping me of the grants I received the previous year. Since I had no idea this would happen until school was about to start, I had to take out more loans that year.

The next year, my sister became independent as well, and once again, my parents made more money. My financial aid diminished further. Just so we're clear, my parents are by no means rich. My family was about as middle of the middle class as you can get. But apparently, they made just enough to choke my government assistance.

On top of this, tuition costs at my school went up. In fact, they went up every year I was in school. Over the course of my college career, the credit hour cost increased by $100. When you consider the fact that I was taking about 32 credits every year, that's a lot of money.

Of course, I didn't really understand most of this until I was done with college. I (technically my mom) filled out my FAFSA, got a tiny scholarship or two, paid for my books out of pocket, and took out loans for the rest. Thanks to some classes not transferring properly, I had to extend college by a full semester, plus an additional standalone class the semester after that. Weeks before I graduated, I would discover that I retook at least three classes that I didn't have to retake. Turned out someone in my college's registrar's office had misinformed me. To put that in monetary value, that's around $5000 $6000 extra added to my college bill.

When it comes to course requirements and transferred classes, I recommend keeping a close eye on your records. Fill out a petition when necessary to demand that the classes you've taken count for specific requirements.

Anyway, my final semester at school, I wasn't a full-time student which meant the countdown to my loan payments started. Once you are no longer a full-time student, you have a sixth month grace period on your loans. When that passes, interest starts compiling, and fast. You know how the Hulk turns into a giant green rage-monster when he gets angry? It's like that. By the time I officially graduated from college, my loans were only a month away from kicking in.

Both sets of loans, that is.

You see, I had forgotten that I wasn't just taking out loans from a bank. When you fill out your financial aid, you can get these things called federal loans. Unlike federal grants, federal loans need to be paid back (hence the name federal *loans*). Since I graduated jobless, I had to defer both my private and federal loans. That means you don't have to make payments, but interest is still in effect. This can get very ugly, very fast. Seriously, I recommend doing everything in your power to avoid loan deferment.

When I finally sorted out how many loans I had, how much I would have to pay, and how much I had already racked up in interest, I wanted to cry. I didn't cry. But I wanted to. Like, really bad. It was a very dark day. I remember standing in my apartment and being hit so hard by the realization of how much I was in debt that I collapsed into a chair next to me.

Then I think I called my mom.

The Bitterest of Pills

Sadly, for many of you, loans will be a necessary evil. If you aren't getting a full ride, and if your parents/grandparents/etc. aren't paying your way, you will probably need to take out some form of loans to go to college in a timely manner. As I mentioned before, there are essentially two categories of loans you'll encounter.

Federal loans are from the government and have smaller interest rates. Private loans are through banks and other financial institutions. These tend to have ridiculous interest rates. Interest rates are like parasites. When they first become a part of you, you don't really notice them. Then, slowly but surely, they start feeding off you more and more, growing to out of control portions as they siphon away your life.

And it's like I said, once you aren't a full-time student, that's when interest kicks in. If you have enough debt, it could be growing by hundreds of dollars per month. Look at it this way:

Once you start paying off your college loans, it's like you are throwing dirt into a giant hole, trying to fill it up. Meanwhile, some evil person is down in that hole, throwing the dirt back out. If what you're putting in isn't substantially bigger than what is being thrown out, you are going to be filling that hole until you're buried in one of your own.

You may graduate with $37,000 worth of debt (the current national average), but by the time you have them paid off, those loans could end up costing you $50,000. And all the while, you will be saying "If only we had listened to Tim and his wise words!"

If only my friend, if only.

And I just want to add, this stuff with loans doesn't just apply to college. Loans, credit cards, debt, mortgages. All of it can get very terrible without you even realizing it. To make it worse, as you grow older, the opportunities to get into debt will increase dramatically. You should always be hesitant to spend money that you don't actually have.

Something to Consider

I was out for coffee with my friend Mitch. We get coffee a lot. Coffee is relatively cheap, and it leaves us with the opportunity to share our thoughts and feelings and other manly things. Since Mitch and I both play the guitar and like to sing, we often dream of being legit musicians. To be honest, I think Mitch could be one. When he plays and sings, the melody sinks into your bones, stirring your body and reminding you that the human soul is a very real thing.

"Sometimes, I just wish I could travel the country, playing music. No home or possessions. Just living off the road with me and my wife."

"Oh yeah?" I asked.

"Well yeah. Don't you ever just want to leave everything behind and do something like that?"

I gave a halfhearted smile as I nervously picked at the cardboard sleeve on my cup. "Almost every day."

"What's stopping us?" I heard Mitch say amongst the thoughts inside my head.

"Loans. Debt. Jobs to pay them. We're stuck, man. We are stuck."

Mitch fell silent.

It was a very suffocating realization, knowing that our current lives could only be so adventurous because of our collegiate lives. Maybe one day I would have my loans paid off. Maybe one day I wouldn't have to worry about this thing called debt.

But in that moment, I was bound, and I had been since the age of 18 when I took that first loan out. When you start taking loans out, make sure you're in it for the long haul. Make sure there is some sort of end game in place. Once you choose that big-time college or university, someone is going to have to pay for it sooner or later. Maybe you'll land a high-paying gig that will remove all of your loans upon graduation.

You can't bank on that though.

Do I regret going to college or taking out loans? I'd say no to the first, and yes to the second. But even now, I'm not sure how one would have happened without the other. I wish I wouldn't have had to take out loans, but I think I had to. Still, I could have done a much better job of tracking and managing them. I could have (and should have) been more responsible. I can't change that. Mitch can't change that.

But if you're still at the beginning of your college education, you can. Please, don't be stupid. Life is much harder when you're stupid. John Wayne said that. He's from Iowa, in case you didn't know.

Here is the best advice I can give on loans: have a plan. Specifically, an endgame-plan. Sit down with someone (parent, teacher, guidance counselor) and set a limit on how much you can take out in loans per year. Once the amount is set, stick to it. If your college costs more than the set amount, pay the difference out of pocket. Most colleges have a pay as you go plan so that you can make monthly payments.

I did that for one semester. I should have done it every semester.

Chapter 3:

Don't Rush Things

"I swore I saw Greg yesterday," I said to my friend Tyler.

"You probably did," said Tyler. "He's taking a 'break' from college."

"Oh yeah?" I replied. "Is he pregnant?"

"What?" said Tyler.

"I mean, is someone he knows pregnant? You know, someone he *knows*."

"No, Tim," said my impatient friend. "Why do you always think someone is pregnant?"

I shrugged. "I don't know why I think a lot of things."

"Anyway, I heard he just wants to take some time off and figure out his life or something."

"Well good for him."

"Are you serious?" Tyler asked.

Suddenly, I wasn't sure if I was. "Maybe?" I finally said.

"Dude," said Tyler, "Don't you know that three-fourths of people who drop out of college never go back."

"Yeah," I lied, "I totally knew that. What a....a bum! And I don't mean the British word for your rear. I mean the American word for worthless human being."

"Right. Pretty much a guarantee he'll be working a dead-end job."

"That's just too bad. How's he ever going to support his kid?"

"He's not pregnant Tim!"

"It's just, I mean, how do you really know?" I asked.

This semi-true conversation that I had back in high school demonstrates two things: how quickly rumors can formulate and how easily made up statistics are believed. While the exact percentage sometimes changed, I heard this statistic over and over when I was younger: the majority of people who drop out of college never go back.

I don't know if it's true. Maybe it is. When used properly, statistics can be great. But in instances like this, I've found that much like standardized tests, they're a bit too broad and impersonal. In the case of college, it's the person that chooses whether or not to go back. Maybe Greg had a great reason for dropping out. Maybe those "three-fourths of people" have great reasons for never going back. I don't know.

What I do know is that it makes a lot more sense for someone who is unsure of college to take a year off than it does for them to go and spend thousands of dollars on something they'll never finish or use.

I'm sure there's a parent who will read this and get upset with me because I'm telling their kid not to go to college. That's not what I'm saying at all. I'm simply saying there's no reason to rush. Modern culture is in such a hurry. Pick a school, pick a spouse, pick a job, pick the rest of your life **right now** before it escapes you. I don't mean to sound preachy, but I've met too many people who hate their jobs, have been affected by divorce, and are in loads of debt (like me).

And so often it's because they chose too fast. Life decisions are so important because they impact your *life*. What you choose will have a ripple effect for years to come. College shouldn't be a shotgun wedding. And just so we're clear, your wedding shouldn't be a shotgun wedding either....

No Regrets. No Looking Back.

I have a sister-in-law named Savanna. When my brother started dating her, the first thing I learned about her was that she was blonde. The second thing I learned is that she was in the running for Miss Minnesota. I was initially quite surprised because Miss Minnesota is only one step away from Miss America which essentially meant that my brother was somehow dating a beauty queen. Though she ended up not quite winning Miss Minnesota, her story remains one worth telling.

Before I met Savanna, I imagined a very stereotypical blonde pageant girl: ditzy, bubbly, wears too much make-up, excessive amounts of pink, the list goes on. I couldn't have been further from the truth. That's what I get for using stereotypes, I suppose. Savanna is smart, responsible, passionate about her beliefs, driven towards her goals, and very blunt. Maybe a little too blunt at times. She also has a phobia of tulle. Sounds like the kind of person that would jump right into the college arena, right? Wrong. She never went to college.

And her life is better for it.

Blasphemy, you say? Listen to the story, and then you can judge. As her high school days were coming to a close, Savanna had planned on attending a school in Oklahoma. Everyone else was heading off to college. Why shouldn't she? Savanna had been a small-town Minnesota girl her entire life. Maybe this was a chance to escape, to adventure and "discover herself", whatever that meant.

When she told other people about it, the college plan sounded great. When you talk about going college, no matter who you are, most people seem to react like it's a great choice. It doesn't really matter if it is or not. But deep down, Savanna felt called to something besides college. Right before she went off to Oklahoma, Savanna changed her mind and ended up taking an internship. It was a bold decision, and one that many probably saw as a step backwards, but from day one of her internship, she knew she made the right choice.

She still moved out of her parents' house. She still discovered who she was. But instead of learning from a textbook, she learned lessons through life.

Once her internship was done, she was hungry for more of life. At this point, going to college felt like a lateral move at best, so she hopped into the pageant arena instead. Competing in various contests took her across the state, allowing her to meet people and impact their lives, even if just for a moment. She also had the freedom to volunteer, helping those less fortunate. Had she gone to college at this point, she would need to be paying for it. To pay for it, she would need a job, if not a career. All of this would have left her with little to no time to help people and experience the world around her.

Many go to college to expand their horizons, but in the case of Savanna, it would have limited her options. She was exactly where she was supposed to be, making connections and following her passions. But there comes a time when life moves on. Like seasons changing, Savanna's time as a pageant girl came to an end when she lost Miss Minnesota. She wasn't too saddened by it. She simply saw it as the chance to start the next chapter of her life.

While doing the pageant thing, Savanna started working part-time at a local clothing store chain. That part time job soon turned into a full-time job. The full-time job turned into an assistant manager position. Finally, the assistant manager title transitioned to store manager. In two years, Savanna had gone from an entry level position to running her own clothing store. That's how long it takes just to get an associate's degree.

But she wasn't just working. It was during this time that she developed her relationship with my brother. That relationship quickly turned into a marriage. After she gave birth to their first child, Savanna decided to take a break from the retail world. Since she didn't have any debts, she could afford to do that. Today, Savanna and my brother have two daughters, one son, and a chubby little dog. They own a house, they have two vehicles, and they still manage to have a little spending money on the side.

College is still an option for Savanna, should she ever feel led to do it. In fact, she has some scholarship money that she earned during her pageant days. But for now, she's perfectly content being a mom, a wife, a church leader, and a part time server at a local restaurant. By the time her high school classmates were landing their first post-college jobs, Savanna completed an internship, opened and ran a clothing store, competed in a state-wide beauty pageant, got married, and had started a family.

And she did it all with zero debt and zero regrets.

Do you have doubts about the collegiate world? Does college sound like a great idea to everyone except yourself? I have good news; a year from now, college will still be ready and waiting for you. I spent about five months choosing the TV I currently own. I looked at different types and brands. I read articles and reviews. I searched stores and scoured the internet. All for a TV. That's more time and effort than many put into choosing a college.

That's not okay.

I realize there's a lot of pressure. Probably too much pressure. Everyone keeps asking you where you're going to go, automatically assuming that you're going to college *somewhere*. Just know that this is a choice that will have a profound effect on the rest of your entire existence. And it is a choice. You don't *have to* go to college. If you do go, it should be because you want the best possible future for yourself.

It's never too late to stop and think about it. Even if you've already started school.

The Best Laid Plans Can Still Come Undone

"I don't know what I want to be," Jackie told me, "But it's not an elementary school teacher."

There I was, in the middle of another conversation about figuring out life. It has become a reoccurring theme of sorts. The night was supposed to have been one of celebration. It was, after all, Jackie's birthday.

Jackie, our friend Wil, and I had gone out for sushi to celebrate. It was my first time eating sushi. I hate almost all seafood, and yet, it turns out I really enjoy uncooked fish. Life's full of surprises. After dinner, we went over to Jackie's place to watch a movie. *Legends of the Fall*. In case you haven't seen it, Brad Pitt plays an impossibly interesting/complex hero, while Anthony Hopkins has a stroke. There's also a giant bear and a brief WW1 battle scene. That more or less sums up the movie.

By the time the credits started rolling, it was just Jackie and me left in the basement.

Somehow, we quickly went from "So what did you think of the movie" to "I don't know what I'm doing with my life".

"For what it's worth," I said, "I think you would be a great elementary school teacher."

"That's sweet, but I still don't want to be one," she responded flatly.

It wasn't hard to see she was frustrated. I couldn't blame her. Jackie thought she had it all planned. Remember that conversation I mentioned earlier with the high school student who would practically be a junior in college by the time they graduated? Yeah, that was Jackie. And true to her word, she had nearly four semesters of college completed when she received her high school diploma.

The next fall, she headed to a local community college to finish her generals for the lowest price possible. A semester later, she was enrolled in a university as an elementary education major. She had planned on being a teacher for a while. She loved kids and she loved when people listened to her talking. It seemed like the perfect career.

Turns out it wasn't.

She wasn't even one full semester into her education classes when she realized it was not what she wanted to do. She didn't like her college, she didn't like her classes, and she had little idea of what she might actually enjoy doing. To her, there seemed to be only two viable options at this point. Either she would push through the next two years of college and hope her attitude towards teaching changed, or she would start from scratch and pursue something else.

Reading it on paper, the right choice might seem obvious. But when you're fully committed and in the moment, change is hard. It's the same reason why people stay at jobs they hate. Why they stay in relationships that make them miserable.

The place you are currently at in life might suck, but at least you know how much it sucks. What if you head another direction, and it's worse? Let me tell you something I've learned firsthand: it's usually not.

If you find yourself doing something you hate, going a direction you don't like, or being with a person who makes you miserable, and an opportunity arises to change that, take that opportunity.

"But Tim," you say, "how do you know it will be any better?"

Because it will be. Because it has to be. It might take a while. It might seem worse before it gets better, but you'll make it through. If your life is miserable, and you're left with the choice of either staying miserable or trying something different, why not try something different?

That's what Jackie did. It was a process. It didn't happen all at once. But over the course of a year, Jackie transitioned from plan A to plan B, and her life is much better for it.

First, she finished off the end of that school semester despite her lack of motivation. Second, she decided since she was so close to finishing her general requirements, she might as well actually finish them. Once you have completed all general classes, you get what is called an Associate Degree. Though an Associate's Degree might not help you launch a career in a specific field, it can possibly give you an edge in certain other jobs. Particularly jobs that require some sort of certified training or technical school.

Also, if Jackie decided she wanted a four-year degree after all, her Associates Degree would most likely transfer to the major of her choice, leaving her with just two years of college to go.

Jackie, however, didn't go on to finish her Bachelors. Instead, she went to beauty school where she learned to be an aesthetician. From there, she landed a job at a salon and spa, giving her the means to leave her parents' house and move into the city. Having changed her life's plans so drastically, Jackie realized just how much control she had over her life. It wasn't long before she made a road trip by herself to Washington state, a place she had always wanted to go.

Finally, about two years ago, Jackie decided to change her life's course again when she moved out to New York City to take up a permanent residence there. I got to hang out with her right before she left, and needless to say, she was very excited.

Nervous, but excited.

She didn't have a job there yet, and she wasn't sure how it was all going to work out, but she wasn't burdened by debt, and she had the qualifications to land a number of jobs. It didn't take long for her to get not one, but two jobs, one of which happened to be at a spa. Now she's living the dream in NYC. Sure, there was a homeless man who used to sneak into her apartment complex, borrow people's mail, and urinate in the stairwell from time to time, but that's all part of her grand adventure.

Speaking of adventures, Jackie ended up marrying a man out in New York, and they have a kid together. All of this might not have ever happened if she wasn't willing to leave her college plans behind.

It wasn't an easy decision for her to make. Jackie isn't the type of person that likes to feel out of control. Making that decision and sticking with it was very hard for her at first. She even clashed with her parents. There was grief, pain, confusion, and a few tears were shed, but when the dust settled, Jackie knew she made the right decision. As she entered beauty school, she rediscovered a passion for learning and growing. She took pride in her work. And she might not know exactly where she will end up, but she has a pretty good idea of what she will be doing.

That's the great thing about trade schools. They train you in a specific area for a specific job. If you want a very specific job, they're a great route to go. Becoming certified is generally cheaper and takes considerable less time than earning a full college degree. If you don't want to take all the extra classes, you just might want to look into trade schools.

Working Through It

"You know," my father said, "I made my...."

"Last school payment a week before graduation?" I responded, staring blankly out the window. "No dad, I didn't know that. Please tell me more. It sounds like a very riveting story. I might even use my writing degree to tell others about it someday."

"I'm just saying," my father said defensively, "It's possible to do."

"Yeah, if you sacrifice any hope of a social life."

My dad scoffed next to me. "I had a social life," he said. "I did things all the time."

I wasn't sure which was weirder, the fact that my dad paid off school while being a fulltime student, or the fact that he had friends and was social. Both seemed about as ridiculous as seeing a horse riding a cowboy.

I always had a hard-enough time balancing just classes and friends. Throwing work into the mix made things much more frustrating. I actually worked a variety of jobs throughout college. Do I regret working when I could have been socializing or napping? Not really. If anything, I regret not working more. Let me be frank. While I understand that many students would struggle working full-time like my dad did, I fully believe that most students should have a job during college.

And all the parents said "Amen!"

There are, of course, exceptions. If you have a full ride scholarship that requires you to maintain a certain GPA or get so much practice time in, feel free to not have a job. Your college is covered, and I'm sure you are putting a lot of effort into whatever you're doing. For the rest of you, get your butt off your couch, hop on your computer, and start applying to anywhere and everywhere. Having a job has numerous benefits, some of which you may not even realize.

The first benefit is simple: you earn money. Maybe you can't pay off all your college as you attend, but you could pay off some of it. One of the few smart decisions I made was paying for my textbooks out of pocket every semester. Any amount of money you can put towards college now, the better you will be later. You can also put some of that money away into savings. That way, if you're not making the big bucks after graduation (and you probably won't be), you have a little padding to fall back on.

Of course, you can also spend some of that money. Students in college like to do things like go out to eat and go to the movies and buy stupid things. A job can give you spending money so that you can do that too. Because trust me, no one wants to hear that you're broke. And no one wants you mooching off them. Get a job.

The second benefit of a job during college: work experience. When you're nearing graduation and you start sending out applications, most employers don't want to see that you've done absolutely nothing for the past four years.

"But I was taking classes!" you cry.

A lot of employers don't care. They want to see some actual activity on that résumé, even if it's being the weekend manager at a Caribou Coffee.

The third thing a job can give you is an extended social circle. It's very easy to get wrapped up in your college's bubble. If you work off campus, you can meet new people. You can have more friends. There are loads of great people out there, waiting for you to meet them.

My final reason to have a job during college? Job security. Having a job during college can easily turn into having a job after college.

When You're Not Ready to Say Goodbye

I had worked with Ericka for about seven months before I started talking to her. I can't exactly say why. I'm generally a friendly guy and she was a very friendly girl. Maybe it's because another one of our coworkers was always trying to set us up (despite the fact that Ericka had a boyfriend). Regardless, I eventually discovered Ericka was great company to keep. The sad thing was, she was about a month out from graduating from college and leaving her "job" behind for a "career".

Much like my friend Jackie, Ericka was going to be an Elementary teacher. She had finished her student teaching. She had completed the curriculum. She was joining a network for substitute teaching. Finally, the time had come for her to give her two-week notice. It was a bittersweet day. Ericka had worked there for four years, and she did a fantastic job. But we all reach times in life where we have to make like a baby and head out.

Her last two weeks of work flew by. Ericka was gone.

It wasn't a month later I was walking into my place of work, and there was Ericka standing behind the front desk. Naturally, I was confused. Happy, but confused. I casually approached, taking a seat in front of her.

"Hey...Ericka."

"Hello Timothy."

"Weren't you done here?" I said.

"I was," she replied.

"And...." I continued.

"And now I'm back."

"I see that," I said.

We both sat quietly for a moment as I expected her to continue speaking. Instead she simply shuffled the paperwork in front of her. Finally, I pushed for an explanation.

"So why are you back?" I asked. "Not that I'm not ecstatic to see you. I'm simply curious."

She sighed heavily. I must have been the 50th person to ask her this. "Because I don't want to be a teacher," she said.

"Do you not enjoy teaching?"

"No," she said, "I love teaching actually."

"Well, isn't that what teachers do? Or did they stop teaching? Do they do something else now?"

"It's not the teaching that's the problem? It's..."

"The kids?" I cut in. "You hate kids. That's understandable. I have mixed feelings about them myself. Dogs, however, love dogs. You should be a dog teacher!"

Ericka looked like she wanted to slap me. "No Tim," she said dryly, "I love kids. What I don't love is the idea of running a classroom. Building a curriculum. Managing and organizing everything. Keeping track of everyone's stuff. I have no desire for it."

"So you're back," I finished.

"So I am back," she confirmed.

"From outer space..." I added.

"Huh?"

"You know, I just walked in to find you here with that sad look upon your face...?"

"Tim, you're so weird sometimes."

I sighed. "It's my burden. Anyway, it's a good thing they love you here. I'm sure your manager took you back with open arms."

"Tim," she said, "it was actually too easy."

Ericka was in a less than ideal situation. She just graduated with a degree she didn't want to use. She liked the basic idea of what she was going for, but got turned off by the details. It's something just about anyone can run into in any given major. Some people might have had to simply suck it up and work a job they hate. Ericka however, had a fall back option.

Because she had worked diligently throughout her college career, she had a steady job that could sustain her. A place where everybody knew her name. Is it what she went to school for? No. Is it what she wanted to do for the rest of her life? Probably not. But for the moment, it was a lot better than scrambling for any job she could get her hands on. It was better than being completely miserable everyday as she carried out a career she despised.

Many will say that life is too short to work a job you hate, and that's true. But life is also generally long enough to briefly tolerate a job you don't necessarily love while you figure out some of the finer details.

I know that doesn't sound very sexy, but I've been broke and jobless and trust me when I say that's less sexy.

As for Ericka, she has since moved on from her job at the front desk, using her connections to earn a position that has taken her across the world. I always see pictures of her on Facebook in some foreign country. I'm not entirely sure what she does now, but I think she's just fine with not being an elementary school teacher.

Finding Work that Works

Throughout my college career, I worked about 6 different jobs. At the time, I was just trying to take what was available when it was available. After seeing Ericka's story unfold, I wished I had done that differently. The jobs I had were to get me by for the moment. It's as though I was in a boat with a hole in the bottom and water flooding in. Each job was this temporary fix, a shoddy patch of duct tape placed across the hole. It would hold for a while, allowing me to sail just a bit longer.

But I didn't need a temporary patch. I needed to fix the freaking hole in the boat. Or just get a new boat altogether. I think I've lost the illustration.

The problem was, I spent so much effort just trying to get through the day that I wasn't ready for tomorrow. On the other hand, Ericka's job ended up being an investment in her future. She got plugged in at the start of college and continued to work her way up the ladder while attending school.

Generally, the longer you work at a place, the more money you will make and the more the place will be willing to work with your schedule. If you can find the right job during your first year of college, you can ride that job out for the next four or five years. Maybe it will even turn into your career. Even if it doesn't, the experience could help you land a career eventually.

Some job experience is better than other job experience. During my two years of post-college limbo, I scoured the pages of the internet looking for any job that could be considered a career. I mean *anything*. Between Craigslist, job listing directories, and corporation websites, I was certain that sooner or later, my super awesome diploma could give me the edge I needed. It turned out almost everyone wanted legit experience in addition to a college education.

I had plenty of "job experience". Unfortunately, US Bank didn't care how well I could park a car. Target Corporation wasn't impressed by my sandwich making abilities. And the handful of marketing positions I found weren't looking for furniture moving skills.

It was during this time that I learned not all job experience is equal. In fact, a lot of job experience is kind of worthless. Valuable job experience includes IT work, office administration, database management, copywriting, and if you're going into sales, sales experience key. I was not going into sales, so my sales experience was also worthless.

However, a college job doesn't have to be all about what experience you get. If the pay is really good, it's hard to say no, even if it won't land you a career later. You can also look into jobs with practical benefits. There was a reason why my dad was able to work so much, yet still get his schoolwork done and have time for a social life. See, he worked in a parking ramp at night. All he did was sit there in the security office. That was it. He basically got paid to complete his homework. Who wouldn't want to get paid to do their homework?

There's one final job you can consider, though it's for the people who don't have to rely on their jobs for much financial support. That is the "perk job". Do you love movies? Work at a movie theatre and see them for free! Want new clothes? Retailers are always hiring. During college, I worked at a Buckle for about 4 months. In those 4 months, my wardrobe and personal style was entirely changed. I didn't really like the job, and it didn't help me land a career, but it carried other long term benefits.

Are there any specific jobs you should avoid? Why yes, there are.

I was in my school's deli, putting together a sandwich for dinner when my friend Pete walked up. From the rose red in his cheeks and the stiffness in his posture, it was clear he had either been standing in a meat locker, or he had just spent a good amount of time outside.

"Walking the streets?" I asked.

"Hustlin' ain't easy," he replied. "I just got back from work."

"Do you sell drugs in the alleyway or something?" I asked.

"Not exactly," he said as I began to assemble a sandwich next to me. "Not at all actually. I go to people's houses and help them save money on oil changes and other car services."

"You mean you sell door-to-door?"

"Yes. Technically. But it's great. I work when I want. I get to walk around and meet a lot of people. And for every sale I make, I make $30. A sale usually takes about 10 minutes, so you can make some really good money."

Now, there should have been a couple red flags that went up here. This wasn't just sales, but door-to-door sales. During winter. In the state of "Minne-so-cold, you wonder why people settled here in the first place". Not to mention the fact that my friend Peter didn't exactly seem to be rolling around in money. But I didn't pay attention to any of that.

I was jobless at the time, and I heard him say that I could set my own schedule and make $30 in 10 minutes. That was enough for me to sign up. A few wasted months later, and I had knocked on hundreds of doors, had a person or two threaten to call the cops, and made about $120 total. What's really sad is that during this time, I passed up a legitimate hourly job because I could *potentially* make more with door-to-door sales.

This is where I learned that guaranteed wages are typically better than potential wages. If you see a job offering that says "you *can* make hundreds of dollars in a few days", it probably means you won't even make a hundred dollars in a month. My advice? Get an actual job with actual wages. If you can legitimately sell stuff and you like to do it, then go ahead and get a sales job.

If you hate sales, DON'T GET A SALES JOB.

All the Wrong Places for All the Wrong Reasons

I used to be a big fan of the show *24*. The main character, Jack Bauer, was a one-man-army who always seemed to make the right calls in tough situations. Naturally, he was incredibly resourceful. One of Jack's specialties was make-shift interrogations. There was an episode where Jack grabs a wet towel and starts stuffing it down a guy's throat, saying that when he pulls it out, the man's stomach lining will come with it.

I don't know if that's anatomically possible, but it made for some entertaining television.

The problem is, torture is very much frowned upon in the real world, and for good reason. The idea goes that when a person is put under extreme pain or pressure, they will say just about anything to make it go away. Start snapping a man's fingers one by one, and he'll shout, "It was Colonel Mustard in the library with a pipe!"

It might seem a bit overdramatic, but the physiological repercussions of torture aren't entirely different from what students experience as they reach high school graduation. You can't walk ten feet without being asked "Where are you going?", "What are you doing next year?", or "What do you plan on doing with that?".

It reaches a point where a person will say just about anything to make everyone shut up.

I started looking at colleges pretty early in my life. In fact, I made my first visit to a college during my freshman year of high school. It was part of this art school conference held at this sweet college in Minneapolis. I showed professors and recruiters my artwork, asked questions, got feedback, and went home with a library of brochures.

Thinking there might be something to the art school scene, I attended the same conference the following two years. My third year there, I took a grand tour of the school where it was held, and it was during this tour that I realized art school was not for me. I liked art, but I wasn't sure I loved art. I was good at drawing, but I wasn't sure I had what it took to become great at it. Really, I just didn't feel like I would fit there or any art school for that matter.

So I walked away from art school.

Now I was halfway through the 11th grade with no idea what I wanted to do, stuck with the mindset that I absolutely *had to* go to college in less than two years. As days turned into months, the questions of what I was doing with the rest of my life came at me more frequently. Everyone wanted to know what college I was going to, what I would study there, and what I would do with that degree when I graduated. As if I was supposed to know at the age of 17 exactly what career I would be working for the rest of my life.

I was a skydiver sailing through the air without a parachute, watching the ground draw closer as I gained speed. And I was helpless to stop it.

To make things worse, everyone else seemed to know exactly what they were doing. They had all sent applications and picked majors. Meanwhile, I was sitting in my room, playing PS2, pretending that everything would work itself out. *Maybe I should just start applying to places at random and think about attending them later,* I would say to myself.

Of course, I didn't do that. I was now a Senior in his final semester of high school who was dead set on going to college despite not having picked one. I hadn't even applied to one. I couldn't admit that to people, though. There was one time when a friend repeatedly asked me where I was going, and I panicked and ran away. No, seriously. I ran out the door, got in my car, and drove off. That strategy worked for a while, but finally things reached a breaking point, and I couldn't take it anymore.

"I'm going to ISU!" I shouted.

Iowa State University was a popular destination for many in my hometown. Though I wasn't a Cyclones fan and had no idea why their school mascot was a cardinal inside of a tornado, I had a lot of friends who either went there or were planning on going there. It seemed like a logical place to go.

"We always thought you might end up attending a state school," my parents said. I wasn't sure what they meant by that, but I smiled and nodded.

"Yep, you know me. I'm all about the state...of Iowa...and its universities."

My friends were pretty supportive too, especially the ones who were also planning on going there. "Oh my gosh Tim," they would say. "We're going to have so much fun next year! I can't believe you're going to ISU!"

"Me either," I would say, and it was true because I had no idea if I would actually be going there.

"Did you officially hear back yet?" they would ask.

"From what?" I would respond.

"From ISU, silly."

"Oh, right!" I'd say with a nervous laugh. "I thought you were asking if I've heard back from Keira Knightley yet. Which I haven't. I write her every day you know, asking her to be my wife and whatnot."

"Tim, I don't think it's ever going to happen."

"Don't step on my dreams, man!" I'd say with a fire in my voice. After a rather long and uncomfortable pause, the discussion would continue.

"So...college?" they would say.

"Well, I mean, obviously I've sent in my application," which was a complete lie, "But I haven't 'officially' heard back yet. My grades are good though, and my ACT score was really solid too so I know I'll be accepted. I'm in like a pigskin. During a football game. Where a touchdown was just scored."

"Never say that again, Tim," they responded.

What I said wasn't all lies. My grades and ACT scores were solid. Had I ever actually applied to ISU, I have no doubt that I would have been accepted. But I didn't. Why would I? I had no intention of going there. Instead, I simply continued to talk about attending there. I did it so much that I almost believed I was going there. Almost.

But as graduation began lurking like a cottonmouth snake in tall grass, I started to feel my lies crumbling. I remember being miserable. What should have been a very fun and exciting time turned into stress and anxiety. I felt as though something was wrong with me because I had no clue what I was doing or where I wanted to go to school. Even if I wanted to go to ISU at this point, it would have been too late to apply.

And I couldn't *not* go to college. If I skipped out on college, I was dooming myself to become a nobody.

Finally, with all my other options exhausted, I sent a last-minute application to a small private college in North Dakota. It was the college my siblings were going to, and they'd take just about anyone who was willing to pay. I was accepted about two months before classes started. To be honest, there was no reason for me to go there. I wasn't interested in any of the majors they offered. I had no desire to live in North Dakota. And even though I had been on the campus once, I had never actually toured the place.

Was it the end of the world? No. But I would have much rather had my first year of college be a decision I made instead of a circumstance that was "forced" upon me. This also started the escalating problem of me having no idea what I was doing while I was in college.

You may have no idea where you want to go to college or what kind of job you want have. That's okay. There's time to think about it. But you do need to think about it and talk about it. Eventually, you have to make a decision. Don't worry, you can always change your mind. Even if you pick a major right away, you can change it.

Pick a college that you want to be at. Take general classes. Focus on your talents and passions. I remember when I started looking at actual classes and majors at the school I ended up graduating from. They got me excited. I actually looked forward to taking them. I knew that I wanted to be an English major because I loved to write and tell stories.

And I knew that if I wanted to be great at writing, I needed to go to college.

I'm not saying every writer needs to go to college. I'm saying I did. Of course, I didn't figure this out till I was a year into college. I transferred. I lost a few classes in the shuffle. That was my price for being unprepared. But even if you're absolutely sure you know what you want to be, I urge you to keep the future in mind. If you're just finishing high school, trust me when I say you have no idea how much you will change and develop between the age of 18 and 24. I've experienced these changes. I've seen them happen in countless friends.

It's easy to think that just because you've reached your full height or you don't wear braces anymore or you can grow a full beard that *this* is it. You see your developmental stage as completed. It's not. You're not there yet. You're still on the journey. And that is a beautiful thing. One great thing about college is how it helps you to grow as a person. If you choose to go that route, it will serve as the bridge between teenager and adult.

If not, then you might find yourself having to grow up a little faster than your college friends. Either way, be aware. Always. This isn't the end. If anything, it's the beginning of the middle.

Part II

Post High-School Survival 101

Chapter 4:

Don't Undervalue Practicality

By the second semester of my sophomore year of college, I thought I had it all figured out. I had just finished Christmas break. I had declared myself an English major. I was taking my first official writing class. I had friends. Surely the dog days were over. My mountain had been climbed, I had planted my flag, and it was time to descend.

Man, I used to be a naïve kid.

Because I finally had some knowledge, I got a little too comfortable. I forgot that there's a difference between knowledge and wisdom. See, when you're comfortable, it's easy to stop being logical. Just because you know where you are and you have a vague idea of where you're going doesn't mean you have a clue on how you're going to get from the one point to the other.

Imagine you're a writer, and you've begun a book. The concept is genius, and the story is riveting. There's a plan in your head for a beginning, a middle, and one heck of an end. You even have cute, witty titles to put at the beginning of each chapter. As great as that is, it doesn't exactly give you a book.

Do you know what each chapter is going to be filled with? Are you going to be able to keep the reader interested? How are you going to transition between each part of the story? You see, writing a story is a journey in itself. A whole lot can happen over the course of writing a book. You could change. The story could change. The world around you can change. By the time you reach the end, your original idea might not make any sense. Maybe you weren't being very realistic when you started this story.

The first writing class I took in college was scriptwriting. By the end of the semester, we had to have completed a one-act play. After some contemplating, I had my story all framed out. The ending was going to be an emotional show-stopper with the main character waving a gun around in a hate filled rage.

It was grandiose. It was dramatic. It was perfect...until I wrote the story that preceded it.

By the time I got to the end, I realized it actually didn't make any sense in the context of the story. Also, it just kind of sucked. I had to scrap it and come up with a completely different one. This wasn't a bad thing. In truth, it was for the best. I was able to come up with an ending that worked for the story because I was willing to move with the story.

And the journey of college isn't so different. Just because something sounds good initially doesn't mean it is. Just because you have a plan doesn't mean that plan won't change. The best advice I can give in planning your life after high school? Don't limit yourself. Dream big. Set crazy goals. That said, you've eventually got to bring those dreams and goals into realistic, actionable steps. Whether you want to or not, you'll have to be practical.

Leaving high-school, a lot of people start undervaluing practicality. This is a mistake. Especially if you're spending tens of thousands of dollars to go to college.

What Do You Want to Be When You Grow Up?

Declaring your major is probably the biggest decision you make in college. It's possible you already know what you want to be. Maybe you've always known. That's fantastic. Others struggle with this decision. A lot. Even I spent most of my freshman year not knowing what I wanted to be.

As I said earlier, you don't have to choose a major right away. But you do have to choose one eventually.

How do you do that? How do you decide what you want to be for the rest of your life?

Think back to when you were a kid, when you weren't burdened with expectations. When the future was something you saw not with fear, but with hope. What did you want to be then? What did you tell your parents you would be one day? What did you like to do? What made you different from the other kids your age?

See, when you're a kid, your mind isn't tainted by the thoughts and opinions of the world surrounding you. Your desires are pure, and you care less about how other people see you. When you think about what you are going to be, you aren't afraid of whether or not you'll be able to be that. You don't second guess the decision.

You know what you love and you say to yourself "Yeah, I want to do that."

And maybe that something was a little ridiculous, but somewhere inside of your ridiculous childhood dreams is a glimmer of truth. A truth that reflects who you are, and what you could do with your life. If you take your childhood aspirations and filter them through your adult sensibilities, you just might figure out what you want to go to college for.

It's like I said. Dream big, but add some practicality. Once you know what you like to do or have some of idea of the person you would like to be, you can start sorting through your options.

Is it Worth It? Can You Work It?

It's easy to get excited about all the majors a college offers, especially if you're looking at bigger universities. Who doesn't want to learn about ancient Greek philosophers or discover the intricacies of African tribal dances? There are majors to meet everyone's interest, and naturally, you should pick a major that gets you excited.

But most of you also have to ask yourself *can I get a job with that?* If you're just going to college because it's free for you or so you can prove to your dad that you're worthy of running the family company, then feel free to take any major that peaks your interest. For those who are going to college so that they can get a job, you need think about the future.

Art history is cool and all, but is it going to land you a job that you actually want? Or more importantly, can it get you a job that pays well and/or one that couldn't be attained without the degree?

This may be the last thing you want to hear, and it might sound borderline contradictory to my whole "chase your childhood fantasies" spiel, but it's something you need to check yourself on or no one else will. For some reason, friends are often scared to inform you that you're making a big mistake with your current course direction.

"That's a stupid major," said no one, ever. It's as if telling someone their major sucks is the worst thing you could ever say to them. At best, a concerned friend will express a few very passive questions regarding your degree.

"So, Egyptian Architecture, huh? That's a pretty...*unique* major," says your friend.

"I know," you respond. "I wanted to pick something different from everyone else because, you know, I'm different from everyone else. I mean, who wants to take classes about business or education?"

"Yeah," says your friend who is secretly majoring in Business with a minor in Education. "Those are such lame subjects. So what are you going to do with your degree?"

"Well," you respond, "You can do a lot of things with it. I could probably work with a museum or historical society. Maybe even break into actual architectural work."

"Oh?" says your friend. "Are architecture degrees pretty universal like that?"

"I don't know," you respond. "I don't really want to be an architect anyway. You know, a lot of jobs just want you to have a four-year degree in something. Why not pick something cool and mysterious?"

I can see where you're coming from on that last point. The idea of picking a major that's completely foreign to you is exciting. But I've found that choosing a major is less about starting from square one and more about enhancing what's already there. Besides, what if you end up hating Egyptian Architecture?

That's the beauty of electives. Every course of study leaves you with credits that can be filled by almost any class. It's up to you to choose what class fills those requirements. That's where you can take something just because it sounds interesting or because you know absolutely nothing about it.

But when it comes to your actual major, the subject that around half of your classes are based on, why wouldn't you go after something that you love *and* that you can use?

Pick a Major, Any Major

The summer before my last year of college, I lived with a couple that I'm friends with. Their names are Steve and Heather, and the story of their relationship is one for the movies. I'm not going to get into that here, though. All you need to know for now is that they met while attending college in North Dakota. Heather went there for physical therapy and went on to become a successful physical therapist.

See, college can actually get you a job in your course of study.

Steve on the other hand graduated with a degree in Air Traffic Control. At no point after college did Steve work at an airport, nor did he have plans to ever work at one. He chose it because it was a very popular course of study at his college and because his dad was in the air force. Neither of those are good reasons for choosing a major.

Upon graduating, Steve worked as a bartender for a few years and then as a salesman for various businesses. Finally, Steve discovered what he actually wanted to do with his life and started his own business. Does his knowledge of air traffic assist him with his job in any way? Nope. To this day, he wishes he would have gone into something business or technology related, two very broad courses of study.

Instead, he has this Air Traffic Control diploma hanging on his wall. It's kind of hilarious. Not to him. Just to everyone else.

Before starting his business, Steve did go and earn his MBA (Master of Business Administration) to get some business know-how. It goes to show that you can turn around even the most random of degrees. Still, since he took no business classes in college, Steve had to work extra hard while earning his MBA. Graduate degrees generally work best when they build on your previous degree.

I should also mention that if you asked Steve, he'd tell you he learned more about business from starting and running a business than he ever did in his business classes. He questions if he should have just skipped grad school and started a business right away. It's not like you need proof of college education to start a business. A lot of jobs, though, you do.

We say that the point of college is to learn, grow, and develop, and that's true. But behind all of that, most of us go to college for that little piece of paper that says "degree" on it. That is an item that cannot be attained without attending college. We seek it so that we can show it to employers and other important people as proof that we have superior knowledge and experience in something.

If you want to learn something cool or interesting, you can read a book, watch a documentary, or explore the depths of Wikipedia. Trust me, I have loads of "knowledge" from Wikipedia. The "random article" button provides endless amounts of fun. You can even take college classes online for free. Websites like Coursera offer actual college classes from big universities, and many of them are free. However, these classes generally won't count on your transcript, and most of them won't help much with launching a career.

There are, of course, exceptions. A website like Codecademy.com legitimately teaches you how to do all sorts of coding, and it does a great job at it. I know this because I've learned a fair amount of coding from there. You won't end up with an official document proving that you know how to code, but you just might leave with the skills to land a job.

The world of post-secondary education is certainly changing, but for many jobs that require special knowledge and training, you need to go to college. That's why I went to college, to prepare myself for my future career. Unlike Steve, my degree was not picked at random. There was a method to my madness.

Why I Became an English Major with a Creative Writing Emphasis

"Home from school, eh?" asked the creepy old lady in the grocery store. Thin, black hairs came out of her upper lip like the first sprouting crops of spring. I didn't recognize her, but apparently she knew who I was. This is what happens when you're from a small town, and you were in everything in high school.

"Yep," I replied, eying the freakishly large amount of cat food in her cart. "Christmas break."

"So what are you studying?" she asked as if we were lifelong friends.

"English. Writing specifically."

"Oh," she smiled, flashing her dentures. "So you're going to be a teacher!"

"No," I replied.

"No?" she questioned as if she had misunderstood me.

"No," I repeated.

"So you're not going to teach people English?"

"No, I want to be a writer. That's why I'm going to school for writing."

"I see," she said as she started to hobble away with her stockpile of Friskies. "Good luck with that."

For some reason, every person I encountered while I was going to college assumed that I was studying English so I could teach English. At no point did I want to teach English. Why would I do that? So I could have a class full of students who didn't want to be there? No thanks.

See, after my art school dreams died, I was a little lost. Since I was a little kid, I had always dreamed of creating and drawing comics. Of course, half of that process involved writing and developing the story. I had tried to start a book a few times growing up. One of them had a dragon in it. I'm not sure I ever got past the second chapter though.

Maybe that's why I never considered going to school just for writing. But even as I entered my freshman year of college, I wasn't exactly sold on what I was going to do. Sure, I had thought about writing. I think I even told friends I was going to be an English Major at ISU, but we all know that was a giant lie.

It wasn't until my first semester of college that the seed was truly sown into my brain.

For that preliminary semester, I didn't actually pick any of my classes. They were all assigned to me, and not knowing any better, I ran with the ones they gave me. One of these classes was Honors English 1. It didn't take long for me to realize that most people were not in Honors English. To be honest, I wasn't sure how I was.

As it turned out, the English class a person was placed in depended largely on how they did on the English portion of their ACTs or SATs. On my ACT, I got a 34 out of 36 in English, which apparently meant I was some sort of rhetoric rock star. While this doesn't do much to woo the ladies, it was enough for me to get into the fancy English class.

Our class was small, and we met in the basement of the library, surrounded by many leather-bound books and the sweet smell of mahogany. Most of the time, we just sat around and talked about "smart things". One day, we took a field trip and the professor bought us all coffee. It was actually the moment I started drinking coffee, so it's a pretty big deal.

In addition to starting me down the road of being a coffee lover, it was this class (and Honors English II) that put me on the path of being an English major.

"You can do just about anything with an English degree," my ridiculously smart professor said. "A lot of people in the business world actually have English degrees. Almost everyone has to read, write, and edit in their jobs, so an English degree can go a long way."

At that moment, I was sold on being an English major. I mean, my English professor was really smart, and he had oddly muscular legs. Why wouldn't I listen to him?

Shortly after, I went online and began planning my college transfer. As I looked at the courses offered in the English (Writing) tract, I actually started to get excited. Fiction Writing. Screenwriting. Creative Non-Fiction. Even Poetry sounded cool. This was what I wanted to do.

I wanted to write better. I wanted to understand stories, how they work, and why they affect people the way they do. With an English degree, I would gain the skills needed to write novels and stories, but I could also attain a real job in the business world so that I could pay rent and bills and stuff.

The whole experience resulted in this beautiful moment of clarity. Everything made sense. I had always loved creating my own wild and extravagant worlds with interesting characters and snappy dialogue. I had always loved entertaining people and getting a reaction from them. And I had always loved a good story, whether it was in a book, a movie, or a video game.

So I became an English major.

I tell this story not so that you will become an English major (though it's way cooler than people make it out to be), but so you know what it's like to choose the right major. If there is one thing I did right during my college experience, it was becoming an English major. I might not have viewed college as a choice, but majoring in English was all my decision. It's what I was meant to be. I have no doubt.

And I did much better in my English classes than I did in any other classes in college. Not because of how good I was at writing, but simply because I cared more about them. That's the power of choice.

I can't tell you how exactly you're supposed to figure out what your major is. But I can tell you how it should feel. You should feel excited. Your passion should start flowing. You might see a line that connects your childhood to where you are now as you realize that *this* is what you're supposed to do. I find it a little poetic that the first college I ever visited was just a couple miles away from the one I ended up graduating from.

And if you're skipping the whole college scene, I would imagine there's a similar moment of clarity out there for you. Or you end up attending a semester of college, and you know almost immediately that it is not for you. We all have to find our own path, I suppose.

For me, I started getting excited about writing classes and Shakespeare. It was kind of weird when it started happening. At the same time, it made complete sense. I think what helped me to finally make the leap though was the practical thought. I wanted to be a writer, which as far as professions go, isn't the most tangible position in itself. But if you look up a lot of authors, even really famous ones, you'll find that they didn't start as a full-time writer. Saying "I'm going to make a living writing books right after I graduate" is almost like saying "I'm going to learn to play the guitar in ten days".

It just doesn't work like that.

Instead, I planned on locking down a real job that would allow me to write. My degree would serve a dual purpose. I dreamed big, but I mixed in some practicality. Unfortunately, I didn't take the practical side as far as I should have. I said I was going to work this "real" job after I graduated, but I didn't do anything to prepare for it.

While an English Degree certainly can get you a job in the business world, it works much better if you have a supplementary degree or actual job experience. In my case, I could have easily taken a business minor of some sort. Or I could have gotten an internship at a business to build up my résumé. Instead, I began a music minor. I loved music, and it sounded good at the time. Sadly, it did nothing for me in the job world, and I never actually finished it.

The point I'm trying to stress is this: you should know what you're planning on being after you walk across that stage and grab your college diploma. When you graduate from high school, you still have time to search and figure it out. When you graduate from college, you really don't. For better or worse, you're kind of tossed into water where you either swim or drown.

It's easy to get caught up in the dream or think that everything will work itself out once you get there. Let me tell you right now, if you reach the point of graduation with zero plan or direction, your dream will mean very little. Be proactive. You want to be a writer? Start writing. You want to work in some cool, thriving business? Get an internship at a cool, thriving business. You want to be a mathematician? Start...calculating and drawing things with protractors?

Whatever your post college plans are, work towards them now. Hustle. Every day. For a lot of people, attending college is a great start But even then, it's only the beginning.

Trimming the Fat

Much like John Mellencamp, I was born in a small town. It's something I'm very grateful for. There's a certain freedom and safety that small towns have, almost as if you were living in a different time period. In small towns, you don't have to lock your house. Kids can go trick-or-treating across town by themselves. You can leave your car running when you run into the store. Heck, I never even took the keys out of my car. Having lived in a metro-area for a decade now, that seems hard to believe.

Another advantage of small towns, in my opinion, is the school systems. While some might find it weird that you know who every single person in your school is, it severely reduces the presence of "clicks". But what really makes small schools great is the fact that you can be in everything. I mean everything.

Let me elaborate. Over the course of my high school career, I participated in football, basketball, cross country, track, theatre, concert band, marching band, choir, show choir, musicals, plays, individual speech contest, group speech contest, mock trial, student council, the school paper, and I rather unsuccessfully auditioned for the Iowa All-State Choir my senior year.

And it was totally acceptable for me to do this. We had starting athletes who would also have starring roles in the school musical. It's how you made friends and memories and expanded your résumé for college. But as great as these extra-curricular activities were, I discovered the world of college is much different.

Don't get me wrong, it's good to be involved in your college community, and chances are, your college will offer some great opportunities for involvement. That being said, don't forget that you are paying to be at college, and the reason you're paying all that money is so you can get a degree. If you are majoring in social work and you are part of a non-profit school organization, that's awesome. If you're a business major, you should probably be involved in Enactus (formerly SIFE) or something similar.

However, if you're working your way through a physics degree but spending all of your free time rehearsing for the school play, you may need to readjust your priorities.

I went to a college that placed a very big emphasis on student leadership and for good reason. Being a leader in something requires you to develop some very important skills. It's also great to go to a college where you can see your fellow students taking up an active role in campus life. But when those commitments start taking away from your academics, from your pursuits of a career, and your opportunities to make money, they start to become a serious problem.

During my college career, I spent three years in student leadership. The first two years were great. They challenged me, connected me to new friends, and gave me the opportunity to help others transition into their college lives. I got to listen to other students, give them advice, and develop some important relationships. My third year of leadership, however, was something I sort of "fell into". It was my last year of college and I found myself as a director of a student organization.

Being a director is a big commitment. And it's not really something you should do because of random chance.

While I had moments of it that I enjoyed, it ultimately distracted me from my classes, my goals, and to an extent, my pre-existing relationships. So much of my time was devoted to planning events and activities that I didn't really have a desire to even attend. I spent countless meetings thinking about all of the things I needed to get done. In hindsight, I think both my studies and the organization itself would have been better off without each other.

It's better to do a few things well than many things poorly.

College is a time to really think about who you are and why you want to do the things you're doing. Make sure your commitments have reasons. Try to find the purpose behind your actions. School activities and organizations can be invaluable when they enhance your current course of direction. They can develop your skills, connect you with similar minded people, and even offer future job opportunities.

But they can also be Sirens drawing you away from your destination. Before you know it, you're completely lost, heading for sharp rocks. Beware.

Of course, activities aren't the only distractions in your college career. There are plenty of things that can take you away from your studies. And if you let them, they will destroy you.

The Second Worst College Student Ever

"So you're writing a book about it?" Mitch said, holding his coffee with both hands.

"So I'm writing a book about it," I repeated.

Mitch and I were out on one of our usual coffee outings at Starbucks when I decided to drop my book idea on him.

"I love it when you write things," he said in his usual tone of affirmation.

"Well, it is what I went to school for. But what do you think?" I asked. "Do you think it's a good idea?"

"I think you should include me in it," he said. "I'm probably the worst college student ever."

I couldn't help but laugh. Having met Mitch my sophomore year of college, I had a front row seat for many of his school-related failings. "I don't know if you're as bad as a guy I know named Ryan. But I'm sure I can find a spot for you."

"Oh cool, Tim," Mitch said, sipping his coffee, "I'm not even the best at being the worst."

Mitch is a great guy. In fact, he's probably one of my favorite people on Earth. But over the course of his life, he's hit a few "stumbling blocks", particularly with drug addiction and rehab. But the real source of Mitch's problems has often been that when he makes a wrong decision, rather than correcting it, he simply lets it play out until its end.

And more often than not, the end hasn't been pretty.

That's what happened with Mitch's college studies. He would choose to avoid his homework or skip out of classes and he would fall behind. Though he was fully aware of the road he was heading down, he would let it continue. Rather than work extra hard to correct the mistake and pass his classes, he would simply proceed to fail his classes. This haphazard style is what led to Mitch being dismissed as an RA in college.

But then it got worse.

My last year of college, Mitch and I became roommates in an on-campus apartment. Mitch had just started a job where he worked overnight shifts two nights a week. The problem was, Mitch had a full day of classes shortly after those shifts got over. Multiple people warned Mitch that he shouldn't take this job because he wouldn't be able to balance the unorthodox schedule.

Mitch did not listen.

Week after week, Mitch would sleep through his classes. Eventually he over-skipped them and thus, got dropped from them. Yes, they take attendance in college. Even if he hadn't over skipped his classes, he probably would have still failed them. He wasn't trying. His mind was not invested in school. It was painful to watch him fail away an entire semester.

He ended up being put on academic probation, leaving him unable to continue school the next semester. By the time he returned to college, he was married with a fulltime job, making classes a much bigger burden on his adult life. On top of that, all of his college friends had graduated and moved on, leaving him a bit isolated in his classes.

Because Mitch didn't take care of the problem right away, life became much harder for him in the long run.

It's so easy to avoid conflicts. Like hitting the snooze button on an alarm clock, you delay them so that you can rest. But eventually, you have to wake up, or there will be consequences.

The harder you work now, the easier things will be in the future. Isn't that part of why you're going to college? So that getting a career and starting the rest of your life is easier in the long run? If you're not ready to work hard and sacrifice, you may want to reconsider being in college.

Why Bother if You're Not Trying?

Failing a college class is a stupid decision.

This is especially true if you're paying for it by yourself. Would you take a thousand dollars and throw it in the garbage? I hope not. Seriously, if you want to get rid of money that badly, you can mail it to me, and we'll just pretend you threw it away. But you're not just wasting money when you fail. You're wasting time. Time is a very precious commodity that you will never get back. To waste time is to waste your very life.

When you fail a required class, you're going to have to sit through all those classes again. You're going to have to do all the homework again. Of course, maybe you didn't do the homework the first time around. That wasn't your best decision. As you sit through those lectures a second time with classmates who are all younger and happier than you, you'll find yourself thinking *why didn't I just pass this class the first time?*

There are a number of "*reasons*" why people end up failing classes.

For Mitch, it was because of work. For others, it might be partying or a romantic interest. Maybe you'll fail a class because you were always "sick" or your teacher was "supes lame, brah". There is an endless list that contains all the reasons people give for failing their classes, but at the end of the day, the large majority are just excuses.

Excuses won't pay your loans or your rent. They won't complete your degree. They won't land you a job you love. And they won't keep you from having to retake that class you probably hate.

So don't waste your life making excuses. Do you think Mitch is glad that he's still in college three years after all of his friends graduated?

"Mitch," I said, wiping the condensation from my cup of iced coffee, "don't you wish you would have passed all those classes the first time around?"

"Ugh," he said, "I'm so stupid."

"You're not stupid, Mitch."

"I made stupid choices."

"We all make stupid choices."

"But I made all the stupid choices."

I set the cup down and flicked the water off my hand. "Well Mitch," I said, staring into his big brown eyes, "those choices can either be the end of you or you can overcome them, and your story will be that much better."

"Dude," he said, raising his hands up and shaking them, "I'm going to have the best story ever!"

I smiled. "That's a good choice."

"But I still wish I would have passed my classes..."

To be the Very Best, Like No One Ever Was

Now that I've convinced you not to fail your classes, let's take it a step further: do a great job in all of your classes.

Even the boring ones.

Even the ones that you struggle with.

College offers a certain amount of freedom. Classes can be skipped (though typically in moderation), reading can be faked, and tests can be crammed for at the last minute. But if you are taking this time to go to college, and someone is spending all of that money for you to be there, why wouldn't you want to put forth some effort?

Do you want to be the person who buys a $2000 guitar and never learns how to play it? Or who purchases $300 boots and never wears them?

Time and again, exit surveys show that college students' biggest regret is not trying harder. After you're out of college for a year or two, you look back and think why didn't I pay attention in that class? Why didn't I do more of the reading? Why wasn't I participating in the discussion?

I was told this countless times while I was in college, and I still didn't listen. I was left wishing I would have tried harder. I wished I would have read everything and asked questions and talked to the professors more.

And not just for my English classes.

Truth be told, I did really well with those classes. But so many of the others slipped through my fingers. Meanwhile, I was spending thousands of dollars on them. What a waste. There will be classes you have to take that you don't want to take. You can either blow them off and do enough to pass, or you can try and actually learn something.

Remember what John Wayne said? Avoid being stupid.

Pay attention. Be smart. *Learn* in the classes you take. Even the ones that you despise. In the long run, you'll be better for it. There's a reason why those required classes are required. Don't forget, you *chose* to go to college.

So act like it.

One Last Thing to Think About

"I just want to do something I'm passionate about," Tyler said. "I want to try and start my own business."

"Then do it, man," I said.

"I'm trying," he said, "But I have loans to pay off. I need to keep a real job in order to be able to pay those. I suppose I wouldn't have that job without my college degree, but I wouldn't need the job if I didn't have this debt."

I paused, contemplated the words that Tyler had just said. "To do what you want to do with your business, would you need your current degree?"

He shook his head. "Not really, no."

I chuckled. "We go to college so that we can get jobs that we need to have so that we can pay off college. That's almost a quote from Fight Club."

The conversation speaks for itself. How much school do you actually need so that you can do what you feel called to do? What's the price you'll have to pay for that? I'm not saying you don't have to go to college. I'm not trying to undervalue the importance of a great education. I just want people to see and understand how easy it is to trap yourself in an unnecessary cycle.

Even when your intentions are good ones.

Chapter 5:

Don't Expect Everything to Work Out as Planned

I was officially a super-senior heading into my fifth and final year of college when the future really started to look hopeful. That summer, I had lived with Steve and his wife Heather. As I mentioned earlier, Steve owns his own business, and he just happened to start it around the time I moved in. In exchange for him letting me live in his home, I helped Steve with his social media marketing business in any way I could. This included writing, graphic design, some very simple video editing, and a lot of Facebook page creation.

There was certainly something exciting about working for a startup business. Late nights around the kitchen table brainstorming and researching. Extended lunch breaks watching through an extra episode of whatever show Steve and I were into at the time. But more than that, I was doing work that used my skills. Clients would complement my sharp, funny writing style. Once, I even designed a logo that made someone weep from overwhelming joy. And all of this left me feeling good and accomplished and fuzzy inside.

I had business cards. I had something to talk about with people. Best of all, I had an actual plan for my post college life.

Business was growing fast, and I had gotten myself in on the ground floor. At this point, it was just Steve, his partner, and myself. Sure, my pay was almost non-existent, but I figured that would work itself out.

There's this moment near the end of the first Matrix where the main character, Neo comes face-to-face with an unstoppable opponent named Agent Smith. Just as Neo is about to turn and run away, he stops and moves toward Agent Smith, ready to fight him. When someone asks "What is he doing?", another character named Morpheus simply says "He's beginning to believe."

That was me. I was beginning to believe that this whole college situation had begun to work itself out, bringing me to this moment where I stared down my demons and went for it with everything I had. In an act of irony, I turned down a position at the same Panera Bread that would turn me down about a year later.

It didn't matter that I was broke or that I would be paying apartment rent soon. This was the dream, right? This was the real job I could work while I did my own personal writing. I didn't really stop to think about the fact that the whole point of the "real job" was to pay my bills while I did my writing.

As I began my fall classes, all seemed right in the world. I was starting my last full-time semester of college, I was working part time for the business, and I was writing my senior project. It was a novella that was more or less a romantic comedy of sorts. But as fall turned to winter, cracks in my current course started to appear.

Projects for work were often sparse, leaving me literally working from paycheck to paycheck. I didn't have that much time to notice because I was very busy with school and leading a student organization that I didn't even want to be a part of. *If I can just get through the semester,* I told myself, *everything will work itself out by January.*

But as the new year approached, I realized that the career wasn't going to pan out as quickly as I needed it to. I began scrambling for other work to hold me by. Of course, this was 2009, and a rather strong recession had just begun to rock the economy, leaving everyone very slow to hire. And since I hadn't ever worked consistently throughout college, my résumé was a little weak in the eyes of those who did have openings.

The spring semester was a bit of a blur. I was only taking one class so I had a lot of free time on my hands. I sporadically worked for a commercial moving company and did a handful of jobs that Steve had for me. During this time, his partner left the business because she needed more money. Even though Steve tried to keep me optimistic about the future, the writing was on the wall.

I was at my parents' house for my last Easter break of my college career when my phone started ringing. It was Steve. He rarely called unless it was important, so I answered.

"Hey Steve, what's up?"

"Well..." he started. His tone was a little off from normal. I was instantly concerned. "There's something I need to tell you. Janet just informed me that she's moving on. I'm buying her out."

Janet was Steve's business partner and one of the main reasons he started his business in the first place. I had been under the impression that she was in it until the end. With her out, I wasn't sure what this meant for the company.

"Oh?" was all I could say.

"Yeah," Steve continued. "Long story short, she was hoping we would be making more money by now than we are. I mean, we've grown fast, but not fast enough for her. So she's pulling out and going back into sales elsewhere."

"Oh..." I said again.

"So, the reason I'm calling is to tell you that, but also to let you know that I'm moving forward with this business. I still believe in it. I'm as committed to it as ever, and I want to know if you'll stay with me. Are you still in?"

I was silent on the other end. I meant to say yes, but I didn't. I couldn't. All of the doubts I had been brushing away suddenly felt much more real. My body may have been on earth, but in that moment, my brain was orbiting Saturn.

"Tim, you there?" Steve asked.

"Yeah, uh, yeah. I'm in. I'm totally in. To the end."

The words were reactionary, like a groan after someone punches you.

There was a halfhearted laugh on the other end. "You know, when I ask a big question like that, and you hesitate, that worries me a little."

"I was just caught off guard, but hey, this is plan A, and there's really no plan B."

Steve and I made small talk for a bit longer, but that was the gist. Truthfully, not much was changing immediately besides the name. Well, that and my workload. What little I had seemed to disappear over the next few weeks until I had nothing. This happened right at college graduation.

It was simply a matter of money and demand. The business wasn't even generating enough revenue to pay Steve, much less myself, and the work that was coming through didn't pertain to me. Finally, things reached a point where Steve and I stopped talking altogether. I don't think either of us meant to. It just happened.

Everything suddenly felt so cheap and empty. I remember one month, as rent was almost due, I looked around my apartment, wondering what I could sell so that I could afford to keep living there. So much of what I had put value into was suddenly worthless.

Graduation was only a month away, and I had no idea what the next step of my life was. It was then that my dad said something very important to me.

"Well son," he said on the other end of the phone, "it's better to work at McDonald's and make money than to have nothing at all."

The truth hit me like a brick thrown at my sternum. He was right. I needed a job, no matter where that job was at. It was then that I thought back to the Panera that I had turned down the previous summer. I had a friend who knew the manager. A few days later, I had resubmitted my application and asked my friend to talk to the manager about me.

This will work, I thought. *I'm in like a pigskin.*

As you already know, that apparently wasn't the case, and I graduated jobless and broke. Why did this happen? After all, I had a plan. But plans always have a flaw. They can always come undone. A variable can change. You can change. The economy can change.

Thinking back to this time in my life, I realize that the problem was there was no back plan. I had no safety net. Nothing to fall back on.

Honestly, this might be the hardest part of the whole college planning process. After all, you're supposed to have faith in the dream. You're supposed to trust yourself and your destiny. You're supposed to believe in the unlikely and really put yourself out there.

Granted, there may come a point in your life where it is all or nothing. Where you lay it all down on the line and pray everything works out. But this was not one of those moments. This was me gambling away my future.

Like I said in the previous chapter, I should have applied some practicality. I should have had a backup plan.

Defining the Backup Plan

In its very nature, a backup plan is a hypothetical situation. A semi-realistic "what-if" if you would. Sometimes you have to play devil's advocate, forcing yourself to imagine scenarios you hope don't come to pass.

"Good news for you, son," my dad said.

"Keira wrote me back?" I asked.

"Who?" he replied.

"Uh, never mind," I quickly responded. "You were saying?"

"When your mother and I die, you'll be set for life."

My eyes went wide. "You're dying!?"

"Everyone's dying, son. It's only a matter of time."

"Now is not the time for scientific technicalities. Are you planning on dying in the near future?"

"Well, no. But if I did, and your mother did, you and your siblings will be taken care of."

"How's that?" I said, furrowing my brow.

"I just finalized our wills with the attorney. Between our various savings accounts, possessions, and life insurance, you and your siblings will be splitting quite a bit of money. You're welcome."

"Well that's...morbid. Thanks?"

"It's not pleasant to think about, but things can happen."

"Now that I'm thinking about it," I smiled, "I wouldn't mind taking care of all my student loans. Might have to arrange some sort of *accident*."

My dad rolled his eyes. "Speaking of your loans, since my name is cosigned on them, you need to get life insurance too."

"But I'm so young," I said innocently. "And fit." As I said the last words, I did my best to flex one of my less than amazing biceps.

My dad looked at my arm for a moment before reeling back and thrusting his fist into my shoulder as hard as he could. My teeth clenched and my eyes went wide as my pain receptors went off like a sparkler.

"You're not invincible," my dad said, smiling and turning away. "Get life insurance."

As healthy and stable as my physical body seemed to be, my dad was right. All it took was one moment of chaos to bring everything crashing down. And it's no different with your life plans. Your plan might be perfect, healthy, and wonderful, filled with rainbows and kittens. You have a major with a complimentary minor, you have your finances, you have a job, and most importantly, you have a dream.

That doesn't mean at any moment that dream couldn't keel over and die.

Depressing to think about? A little. But look at my own plan. It came unraveled over the course of four months. *But there were red flags!* You cry. That is true, but we rarely see the signs and bad omens when we're living in the dream. We're blinded by bliss. We are consumed with the master plan. We tell ourselves it can't fail in the same way young people believe they will never die.

Dreams may be unkillable, but plans? Plans are fragile. They're shortsighted and limited. More often than not, your perfect plan is far from perfect, and before you know it, the plan dies altogether.

This is a possibility you should entertain during college. This is where you create the backup plan. Because sometimes, the world around you changes. Or it was never what you thought it was in the first place. Or you weren't really the person you thought yourself to be.

Everything You Ever (Thought) You Wanted

The funny thing about plans falling apart is that it usually doesn't happen until the plan is set into motion. It would be nice if you knew right from the start whether or not something was going to work out, but the future is not so easily predicted.

All of us find ourselves wanting. There are these things that we see and desire, and for whatever reason, we dream of a day when they are ours. Even if they're completely unfamiliar to us. Sometimes these are small things.

When I was a young boy, I desperately wanted a remote-controlled car. I think every boy does at one point or another. The commercials made them look life changing, as though the world around you would suddenly morph into this jungle-like obstacle course. Finally, I got one, and it was the best day ever.

For about an hour.

After I took it outside and attempted to recreate the various action sequences I saw on TV, the little R/C car came up short. Actually, it failed at almost everything I tried. After driving it around for about 30 minutes, I found myself completely bored and disenchanted. I took it inside and never touched it again.

Here was this thing that I had wanted for so long, and once I had it, I realized it wasn't what I thought it was. I had these unrealistic ideas and expectations. I'm sure there are hundreds of thousands of boys every year who get remote controlled cars and love them. I wasn't one of them. I thought I was right up until the moment when I held one in my hands.

It's a hard lesson to learn for a little boy, but an important one.

Even with all the dreaming, hoping, planning, and class taking involved with college, you may find yourself at the end with everything you thought you wanted, only to find you never wanted it at all.

I was sitting with a group of high school students I helped mentor when my friend Nicole started to share her story. Having an extensive theatre background, Nicole was great in front of people. She was funny, spontaneous, confident, yet very natural and true to herself. She was also great with kids.

It made complete sense that she wanted to be an elementary school teacher. So she became an ELED major. By the end of her college career, her life seemed perfect. Her classes had gone great. Her student teaching was almost done. She had just married the love of her life.

Having attended her wedding, I can attest that she couldn't have looked happier.

But underneath her perfectly practiced smile, something deeper started to stir.

"I would wake up in the morning," she said, "And I wouldn't want to get out of bed. I didn't want to be a teacher. I felt alone and away from my family. I had no idea what I wanted to do with my life, and I didn't feel like I was good for anything."

She paused as she let the words hang in the air. It was one of the few moments I've seen her not smiling. Nicole stared at the ground in front of her, reliving the dark emotions she had recently been going through.

"I had everything I thought I had wanted, and I was miserable. Some days I just cried. For no reason. I didn't ever reach a point where I wanted to take my life or anything like that. Don't misunderstand me. But if the world suddenly ended, I wouldn't have minded at all."

Even as the words were still leaving her lips, something inside me shook. A sudden flashback of memories came over me, and I realized I knew exactly what she meant. Our situations were quite different, but the inner feeling was the exact same. The complete and utter lack of purpose. The sense that everything you had ever believed was a lie.

It isn't the end of the world, though you'd swear you can see it from where you stand.

But if you take a look at everything that went wrong, you realize you now have a better idea of what you want to do with your life, of who you want to be. Your vision is clearer. I have a friend who got very, very close to marrying someone before breaking it off. It was one of the hardest decisions of her life. Even though she knew it was the right decision, she struggled afterwards. Had all that time spent with her ex been a waste?

Then she sat down, and she wrote a list of everything she wanted in her future husband. The more she wrote, the more she realized why her previous relationship hadn't worked out. She realized the qualities of a person she truly valued, and she hadn't realized how much she valued them until she dated a guy who lacked them.

With her list in mind, she opened herself back up to the dating world, and guess what? I attended her wedding last year. She found the man of her dreams, and she couldn't be happier about it.

How do you know what you need until you feel a hunger for it? Can you say you hate supreme pizza if you've never actually eaten supreme pizza?

As I said before, it's a hard lesson, but a very important one that you *will* learn in some form or another. Maybe it will be through college. Maybe it will be through a relationship. Had Nicole not tried to be an elementary school teacher, she might have kept wishing she was one. She might have spent the rest of her life dreaming of being a teacher, when in fact, it was the last thing she wanted to be.

Nicole didn't have much of a backup plan in place, but she did have friends and family around her to help her through her tough time. She realized that somewhere out there was something she would love to do. And maybe her college degree could still help her attain it.

The question is, where do you go from a place like this?

There's no easy, one size fits all answer. When you spend years of your life heading towards a goal, only to realize upon arrival that you never wanted it, things get confusing. The best thing you can do is to keep moving. Don't stop. Don't curl up into a ball, praying that the world will just end. Stand on your feet, and push forward. You haven't reached the end. It's just a curve in the road.

Start volunteering somewhere. Get a new job. Write a book. Learn kung-fu. Do something, anything, or you will go crazy. College builds up all of these hopes, dreams, and ambitions, and if you don't find some sort of outlet for them, your very soul will explode.

This is where a backup plan is nice. I had a friend who worked at a clothing store during college. They loved him there and told him that once he earned his degree, he could be hired on as a manager. Was it what he really wanted to do? Nope. But he always kept that option there, just in case.

Maybe your backup plan could be more school. A Master's Degree is pretty prestigious, and if you aren't afraid to hit the books (and rack up a little more debt), it is definitely an option to consider. Even if you finish with a college degree you hate, you can turn it into whatever post-grade degree you want.

Remember Steve? He went from air-traffic control to business. That's proof that pretty much anything is still possible in the post collegiate world.

And Now We Play the Waiting Game

If patience were a guy, he wouldn't have many friends. Not that it would be his fault. If anything, Patience would be a super awesome person, always having the best intentions for his friends. Patience would be encouraging and optimistic, telling people to ease up a bit and just relax. Good things rarely come quickly, after all. Even though he would always tell his friends what they *needed* to hear, it would rarely be what they *wanted* to hear.

Eventually, Patience's friends would leave him, calling him a waste of time. They would say things like "You think you're better than me or something?"

And I don't really blame them for thinking that. I'm not a big fan of patience myself. I want things now. *Right now.* In the palm of my hand. I suppose I can blame Netflix, Spotify, Google, and 4G data for that. Today's world is a breeding ground for impatience.

When you were a baby, you cried until you got what you wanted. No matter the time of day, if you cried long enough, someone eventually gave in. After all, you were just a helpless little baby. People fed you, changed you, played with you, and tucked you into bed.

Maybe they even read you a nice story of a boy who graduated from college and received the job of his dreams right away without experiencing seasons of soul crushing doubt and disappointment.

But once you reach adulthood, people don't really care about your crying. In fact, some of them might tell you to just shut up. Or they'll passive aggressively tell other people how they wish you would shut up. That's probably what I would do.

Or I'd just write about you, and pretend what I wrote wasn't about you.

You reach a point where crying doesn't work anymore. It doesn't make things happen faster, no matter how many tears you shed. And you'll realize that sometimes you just have to wait. Sometimes you have to be best friends with Patience, even if he comes off as a pretentious d-bag.

Just because you're not working where you want to right now doesn't mean you won't be some day. The thing that drives so many people to college is the desire not to settle. We don't want an ordinary job or an ordinary life.

We want more of what this universe has to offer. We dream big.

Turns out, the bigger your dreams are, the harder you're going to have to fight for them. Whether you have a job or not by the end of college, just think of how far you've come. Think of how much you've accomplished. Think of how much more you can do.

You're just getting started, after all.

Once you've convinced yourself of what you can do and what you can become, it's time to convince the world.

Everything You Are, Line by Line, in 11 Point Font

Despite my best efforts to remain optimistic, I knew my post-college plans were dissolving like flushed toilet paper. It was time to actually use my résumé that had been sitting on my computer for the past 2 or 3 semesters. First, it needed a little work. I hadn't really made it for job hunting purposes. Lord knows I wasn't thinking about starting a career when I wrote it.

I still have an entire year and a half to sort out this minor detail, I apparently thought at the time.

No, the résumé was for a class. One of the first things I learned about résumés is that there is no universal standard for them. They can be formatted in infinite ways using fonts well beyond Times New Roman. They don't have to be double spaced. Some people put pictures on their résumé. Some use colored paper. You should make sure they're readable, of course. I decided that 11pt font was a good size.

But really, the formatting is a pretty minimal part of the résumé. What matters most is what it says about you. With a résumé, you have to take the most relevant parts of your professional life, and force them into one cohesive document. You need to make yourself sound seasoned and knowledgeable in a way that's applicable to the job you're desiring.

"There isn't a 'right' way to draft your résumé," my teacher said to us, "But I suggest you keep it to one page. And for the love of all that is holy, make sure there are *zero* typos or errors."

These are two very important pieces of advice regarding résumés. The typo one is obvious. The length is a little more debatable, but here's my take on it: If you're just finishing college, you probably don't have that much experience. Certainly not enough to justify a two-page résumé. I don't care how many places you've volunteered or interned at. I suggest you do everything you can to cram it onto one glorious, concise, and typo free page.

But Tim, you think in your delicate little head, *who are you to say what makes a résumé good?*

Funny you should mention that. You see, with my big-boy job that I now have, I've had the pleasure of participating in the hiring process. We were recruiting an entry level writer/marketer, and I looked over all of the résumés of the serious contenders. In total, I viewed around 15-20, and the large majority of them were one page. The ones that went over had little reason to go over, and I judged them accordingly.

Let me tell you another thing about the résumés I received. Most of them were incredibly boring. They started to bleed together in the same senseless dribble like:

- Goals: Establish brand by providing superior information.
- Skills: Computer use and typing.
- Strengths: Professionalism.

I mean, professionalism? Really? That's what you lead with for strengths? If you're applying for a job that requires a résumé, I would hope professionalism is a given. As for the rest, I'm going to assume that if you're applying for a writing position, you know how to type and use a computer. And no offense, but I don't really care what your goals are.

Some people have a goal that they're going to visit the moon someday. It doesn't mean they will. They probably get sick from just going on a tilt-a-whirl. When someone is looking to hire you, they care more about what you've actually done than what you dream of someday doing. The résumés that stood out to me were the ones who had legit accomplishments. The people I noticed were the ones who had unique or above average skills.

You only have so much room on a résumé. Don't waste it with information that an employer already assumes to know about you.

There's a writer named Jon Acuff who worked eight jobs in eight years. And I don't mean McDonald's, Starbucks, and those type of jobs. I'm talking grown-up, career type jobs. Needless to say, he sent out a lot of résumés in his day. It was during this time that he learned something very valuable about résumés.

After sending his résumé to one particular employer, the hirer responded saying that they were tired of seeing people list their goals. He didn't care what people were planning on doing. He wanted to see actual proof of their abilities. So, Jon took his résumé, deleted his goals and replaced it with a section called "Results". It was the first thing he listed after his contact info. Written there was the most notable achievements he had made with his life.

Then he resubmitted the résumé, and guess what? He got the job.

I read about that after I had sent my own résumé to about 30 or 40 different job openings. At this point, I hadn't even received a call or an interview, so I figured it was worth a shot. I took my résumé, removed one piece of job experience that didn't really matter and added a section labeled "Results". This is what it said:

I was an original member of one of the first social media marketing companies in the Twin Cities. I single handedly ran a blog that had over 30,000 views in less than a year. I currently operate ThisBlankPage.com which was designed, built, and written entirely by me. I was recognized as being one of the best writers at my University. I have written web content, blog posts, news articles, books, plays, and everything in between.

Doesn't sound too bad for a guy who had no real professional experience in the fields he was applying for. But everything I said was true. When I ended up applying for my current job, this was listed at the top of my résumé. And when I was hiring for the position at that same company, I wished that all the applicants would have led with something like this. That's great that they volunteered with United Way or that they were in charge of their school paper or that they interned with some agency.

But what had they really done? What had they really accomplished?

When you're living your college life, I encourage you to accomplish things. Don't just set goals, but actually achieve some. Take initiative. Create something that's your own. And when it's time to draft your résumé, talk about it. Lead with those things. With the best things. The stuff that makes you stand out from the sea of boring résumés that you're competing against.

You only have one sheet's worth to make a complete stranger understand who you are and why they should pay you. That's not easy to do. Even for a writer. Getting a job can be very hard. If your résumé sucks, it's nearly impossible.

Accomplish something, and then talk about it. Tell it to the world. That's how you get the job you want. That's how you beat the competition. Of course, a willing attitude and a few connections helps too.

Taking Opportunities

With graduation getting close, I knew I had to find a place to live. Tyler, one of my high school friends, was eager to move up to the Twin Cities area. We decided we were going to be roommates and take on life in the metro together. Problem was, Tyler didn't have a job yet. I mean, I didn't either at the time, but I had been living here for a few years. I had planted some roots.

Tyler, on the other hand, was coming straight out of a college in another town. He was looking for a teaching job. Considering the plethora of schools in the Twin Cities, there seemed to be plenty of opportunity. And until he found a full-time gig, he could at least sub. But after a few months of searching, calling, and applying, Tyler was no closer to having a fulltime job.

That's when a job about thirty minutes from our hometown came up for grabs. Since it was so close to the school district we grew up in, our high school principal was able to give Tyler a glowing recommendation. Also, Tyler would be able to live with his parents for a while, saving him considerable money while he ironed out his finances and loan payments.

A few interviews later, and Tyler had the job. The bad news was that I lost him as a roommate, and I *almost* ended up with a Craigslist roommate named Spencer (#strangerdanger). The good news was Joey moved in instead, and Tyler went off to begin his career. Happy endings all around!

Sure, Tyler left his hopes of living in the "big city", but he wasn't too broken up over that. After all, he had a job now. The job he went to school for. The job he worked so hard to get. You may find that your initial job isn't exactly what or where you imagined it to be. Maybe it doesn't pay quite as much as you hoped.

But if you know it's the job you've been working for, go and get it. Think of it as that first step towards something better. Two years after taking that job, Tyler found himself taking a position at a different school.

One that, to him, had a more ideal location. Had he not taken the first job, he might not have had a chance at the second.

You never know where one opportunity might lead you.

Look at actors. Even the most famous ones often start off in cameos, commercials, awful horror films, or failed TV shows. The start of their career consists of *almost* getting a big part or having their entire role cut from a film at the last second.

But they keep at it. They keep going to auditions and reading scripts and doing everything they can to get noticed. And finally, they get that part that shows their skills to the world. Finally, they break through that barrier and emerge a star.

You might not ever end up famous or world renowned, but the journey to your own career isn't so different. Sometimes actors get lucky and catch a big break early on. Maybe you'll be one of those people, grabbing an awesome job straight out of college.

Or maybe you'll have to endure some crappy roles. Be patient. Work hard. Take opportunities. You'll get there. Tyler did. I did. You will too.

Finish Strong

As much as I made mistakes throughout my college career, my last year of school was easily my worst. First semester wasn't so bad. I stayed busy with my classes and leading an organization that I didn't really want to be in. Since I was living in an apartment now, I had to pay monthly rent. I'm still not sure how I did that without a job, but I did.

Then came second semester.

Second semester, I only had one class. Spanish 2. I had to take Spanish 2 in the spring because it wasn't offered in the fall. Of course, I didn't really know that until it was too late. Granted, I didn't actually have to take Spanish at all. If you don't take two foreign language classes, you graduate with a Bachelor of Science instead of a Bachelor of Arts. They're pretty much the exact same thing.

But since I had already taken Spanish 1, and I had no real job lined up at this point, I figured I might as well take Spanish 2. So there I was, the guy with one class and no real job. I started working part time for this commercial moving company, but work was sporadic. Enough to pay the rent and not much else. To be honest, I don't know what I did with my life during that semester. It's a giant, wasted blur, which is sad because I could have accomplished so much in that time. I could have used the free time to finish strong and get the next chapter of my life setup.

Instead, my college career ended with a whimper.

Maybe I was afraid to let go of my college life. Maybe I wanted to remain carefree while I could, before life's expectations and responsibilities kicked in. Or maybe I was just an idiot. I didn't know that college graduation is completely different from high school graduation. High school graduation carries natural momentum with it. There's so much hype, attention, energy, and possibility.

High school graduation automatically catapults you into the next stage of life, regardless of where you're going. But college graduation just kind of dumps you out. If you're unprepared, it feels less like you're moving on and more like you're being evicted. I couldn't stay, but I wasn't ready to leave.

So I finished poorly. I got turned down for a high school job while driving to my college graduation. Rather than declare my excitement about my graduation to everyone, I was scared to bring it up. If I brought it up, people would ask questions.

What are you doing?

Where are you going?

How are you going to get there?

I didn't have answers. I wasn't ready. I'm fairly certain there was an instance or two where I pretended like I was still in college. I hope that from reading this, you'll make sure you are as ready as you can be should you graduate from college.

You can never be fully prepared. There will always be unexpected variables and happenings. But you can at least try. You can plan. You can do everything you can to finish strong.

Head into your graduation at a full sprint. If you're skipping college, skip it with confidence and energy. Move with such a force that nothing can stop you from your next step in life. If someone who was about to graduate from college approached me and asked "What should I do?", my advice would simply be this: Finish strong.

Well, that and have fun.

Chapter 6:

Don't Forget to Have Fun

I wasn't exactly sure what time it was, but it was early enough that there was no hint of the sun on the horizon. From the reflecting moonlight, I could make out the eyes and teeth of those huddled around me. They were shivering. So was I.

It was the middle of fall in Minnesota, and here we were on the beach in swimsuits, waiting to jump into the frigid waters before us. A "devotion jump" they called it. Wake up early. Jump in a lake. Bond with the students from your residential hall. How did this ever sound like a good idea?

Our Resident Director and his assistant stood before us, each of them holding these massive broadswords that looked like they came from the set of Braveheart. It was hard to hear their voices over the gusts of cold wind that came from the lake. They talked about unity. About service. About devotion.

Then they each stood on opposite sides of the crowd, plunged their swords into the sand, and charged past each other, forming two deep lines. That was the signal. A hundred or so of us charged forward, screaming and chanting as we made our way to the lapping waves.

The water hit my skin like an army of open hands slapping my exposed flesh. But I pressed on. The rocks beneath me poked at my feet, yet I kept running. We all continued until we were submersed. Some went further than others, swimming out, trying their hardest to look as though they weren't experiencing the beginnings of hypothermia.

Then all at once, we headed back. Some were screaming from the cold water and the rocks. Others were laughing hysterically. We all quickly grabbed our towels and ran to our respective cars, cranking the heat as fast as we could. Once we got back to the college, there was hot chocolate for everyone who jumped in.

We all stood around for a bit, sipping chocolate and laughing at how dumb we were for doing what we just did. Then everyone either headed to their morning classes or back to bed. Even though I had a morning class, I had planned to skip it. That was the only way I was going to get up before 6am to jump in a lake.

Generally, it was advised that you save your class skips for days when you were sick or out of town. I was neither. But as I look back on those events that took place about 8 years ago, I know it was the right decision to skip class and jump in that lake.

Because sometimes, you just have to have a little fun.

Some of the Best College Advice I Ever Received

If you reach the end of your college career, and can't remember a single time you pushed all of your responsibilities aside to have a little fun, you did something wrong. You missed out.

College is a time to take some risks. To get out of your comfort zone. To do something reckless.

It's the best time to do things like this. After all, you have all the freedoms of an adult without a lot of the responsibilities. But these times of adventure and mindless abandon are best left to the *moments*, not the day to day lifestyle. Life is lived through a linear progression, but it's very often remembered in moments. And how you live those moments will define how memorable your college life is.

I was sitting in our college's auditorium. The speaker on stage was reflecting upon her time in school. One night, she was buried in homework when a group of friends came to her and said they were going on an adventure. Instantly, she felt torn. Her schoolwork was important. After all, it was the reason she was at college. But the opportunity for adventure was unique. It was a chance for something greater to happen.

Ultimately, she pushed her homework aside for the moment and went with her friends on the adventure. Today, she has no idea what her homework was about. She can't remember if she finished it, or even what class it was for. But the adventure she had that night will stick with her for the rest of her life.

Then she looked up to the auditorium full of young adults, and said "When moments like these come along, choose the adventure. Choose to spend time with your friends, to sacrifice sleep for the ones who mean a lot to you. Don't get so caught up in school that you miss life happening around you."

That was a story I remembered every time a friend approached me at the last minute and asked me to do something, and my college times were so much better because of it

Contradictions

You might be thinking *but doesn't that go against everything you just said in this section?*

What about being practical? Responsible? Remembering the reason we're going to college?

It all fits together.

Once you're done with college, there will be many of your friends you will never see again. You might move across the country. They might move across the world. You'll all be tied to jobs that you can't skip just because you feel like it. In college, you're provided with certain moments and opportunities to be "irresponsible" or "crazy" in a way you simply can't afford to be in the real world.

These moments are rare. They are precious. And because of this, it's irresponsible not to take them. It's impractical to say no to the adventures.

I'm not saying you should be like Ryan, the worst college student ever. Every day isn't a party. Your reason for college isn't to escape your normal, everyday life. But you shouldn't be so isolated from the rest of the world that you're afraid to have a little fun.

There's a time and place to go on your adventures and maybe even to make a few mistakes, and I think you'll know them when they come. You don't want to finish college and say "I wish I wouldn't have done that", but you also don't want to say "I can't believe I *didn't* do that".

There's a balance, and I encourage you to find it. Otherwise, you're bound to go crazy.

Part III

The Beginning of the Rest of Your Life

Chapter 7:

Don't Think It Will Be Easy

The girl shuffled the loose papers in her hands, studying them carefully to make sure nothing was missed. She was young, and it was obvious she hadn't done this often. But she was nice, and very friendly. I could see why they made her a manager.

"So you have restaurant experience?" she asked.

"Yeah," I said. "I worked at a pizza place, a Chinese restaurant, a school cafeteria, and a family diner."

She raised her eyebrows. "Wow, that's quite a bit."

"Definitely worked my fair share of jobs..." I bit my lip. "Not that I bounce around from one to the other. I'm always committed. The Chinese restaurant was a temporary job I had in the 7th grade. The cafeteria was only while I was at school. I left the family place because I graduated high school."

"You had a job in the 7th grade?"

"The owners were our neighbors. My dad got it for me. One day, he walked over there, and when he came back a few minutes later, he informed me that I had a job. Let's just say I was thankful that it was temporary"

"What about the pizza place?" she smiled. There was the smallest of gaps between her front teeth.

"It burned down."

"Oh, sad!"

"It was sad. Probably the best job I ever had."

"I'm guessing you didn't start the fire."

"Nope. It was always burning since the world's been turning."

The manager cocked her head to the side in confusion. I realized she might be too young to know who Billy Joel is.

"Never mind," I said.

"Right," she said. "So why did you apply at Panera?"

"I'm friends with one of your manager's neighbors. They mentioned you might be hiring."

"Cool," she said. "Are you in school right now?"

"Actually," I looked down, "I just graduated from college."

"From where?" There was excitement in her voice.

"North Central University."

"Oh my gosh! I want to go there when I graduate!"

That's when the truth hit me like a roundhouse kick to an unprotected face. I was a college graduate who was undergoing job orientation by a high school girl. I had never experienced such cruel irony and hoped I never would again.

Allow me to get you up to speed on how I reached this point.

A week or two after I received the voicemail from Panera telling me that they weren't hiring, they called back to tell me they actually were hiring. *Hurray!* Apparently two of the people they were about to hire fell through at the last minute. I didn't really care. I had a job just in time for college graduation. At the moment, that seemed like enough.

Fast forward a week from me being hired and here I was being oriented by this 18-year-old blonde high school student who was still a month away from earning her diploma. I couldn't afford to have pride at the time. I couldn't afford to have much of anything, truth be told. If I didn't take this job, I would have no choice but to move back home.

And I would *not* move back home.

I had decided that long ago.

If I wanted to be in the Twin Cities of Minnesota, I needed this job. I needed to let this little girl tell me what to do. I needed to put a hat on my head and an apron around my waist and make sandwiches. Any glamour that remained in my idea of college graduation died on this day.

People had mentioned that my first post-college job probably wouldn't be anything amazing. They didn't say it could be borderline embarrassing. And they left me with the impression that it would only get better, that this would be the low point, the hardest part. They said that life would get easier from here.

Little did I know it was going to get worse before it got better.

Welcome to adulthood: where the piper comes to collect on all of your mistakes.

The Birth of an Adult

Remember step 1 of life's checklist?

It was birth. The blessing of birth is that you don't remember it. You don't remember slipping out of the womb or having the cord being cut from your bellybutton. You can't recall kicking and screaming as the doctor pulls you from a pool of body fluids and lifts you into the air Lion King style. It happened, but you didn't really have to *endure* it.

Being birthed into adulthood is a bit of the opposite because when it happens, you will be very aware of everything. Every feeling and emotion. Every pain and struggle. There's no doctor or nurse to guide you along. It's just you and the world.

And your personal baggage.

When you're born as a baby, you're given a clean slate. When you reach adulthood, the life you lived prior to it doesn't suddenly go away. Physical habits, emotional scars, financial mistakes. It all comes along for the ride.

In high school (and even in college) it's easy to think your choices are free of serious consequences. As if your decisions don't have long term effects until you become an adult. Trust me, once you become a teenager, your decisions start to make some serious ripples in the sea of life. You might not see them right away, but give them time, and those tiny ripples will turn into a tidal wave.

The everyday choices you make right now will have consequences that you will have to answer for some day.

The Truth About Debts

In the ancient world, if a person fell into hard times or accrued too much debt, they could put themselves into servitude in order to work off their debt. It was generally considered a last resort as it involved giving up your freewill until the debt was paid.

There's some irony at work here. By *choosing* to follow this path, people ultimately gave up their power of choice. This tradition would continue for centuries, turning into bond slaves and indentured servants, Though the act of "debt bondage" is no longer around in much of the modern world, this idea is as alive as ever. As I said, when we make choices, those choices have consequences, and we can become bound to those very consequences like ancient servants to their debts.

This is another reason why it's important to see college as a choice, especially if you're paying for it yourself. Whether you use your degree or not, it is a financial point of no return. Sure, you could always declare bankruptcy, but once again, that has consequences of its own. They're pretty serious from what I understand.

I would recommend not declaring bankruptcy.

What it Takes to Survive

I started working at Panera as a last resort. I had a hefty financial debt that I had to pay. And since I chose to live loosely with my finances prior to that, I didn't have any sort of savings to fall back on. I needed a job immediately, so I went to Panera. I went into work at 6am with a hat on my head, a nametag on my shirt, and a smile on my face, working as hard as I could in hopes of making more money.

Though I rose faster than any other employee there, it wasn't enough.

"I need to leave work a little early today if that's okay," I said. I had been working up the courage to say that over the first four hours of my shift.

"Okay..." my assistant manager trailed off. "What's up?"

"I have a job interview." I caught the subtle widening of her blue eyes. "Not like a replacement job. A second job. I need a second job, and I'm hoping this will be it."

"Oh," she said, fiddling with a pen in her hand. "Just so you know, we're making sure you're getting a full 40 hours every week."

She tried smiling. She wasn't particularly talented at faking smiles. Neither was I.

"I know," I said, trying my best to look enthused, "and I appreciate it, but I have debts, and someone needs to pay the Bank of North Dakota a lot of money. So I need to throw a few more hours into the mix."

She paused, nodding slowly. "I understand. We will get you out of here early."

"Thanks," I said as I took my plate of food over to a table for my break. Not five minutes passed before the general manager was my table.

"Hey there Mr. Snyder," he said with a big smile on his face. He was much better at faking smiles. "I hear you got an interview you need to leave early for."

"Yeah," I said, not quite making eye contact with him. "I hope that's okay. It's just a secondary job. Need a little extra money. School debt, man. You can't shake it. It's like, uh..."

"Children?" my boss asked.

"I'm not sure that's the sa...sure. Just like children."

We both sat in awkward silence for a moment. Obscure music played from the speakers above us.

"Anyway," my boss continued, "I just want you to know that you've been doing a great job here. I really appreciate the work you've done. I know it's not the highest paying right now, but I really think you could go somewhere with it. I'd say you are definitely one of our top employees."

My brow lifted. I had been working there around two months, and I was a top employee. Apparently. I wasn't sure if that was a testament to my work ethic or a knock against the staff that had preceded me. I decided it was the former.

"Thanks boss," I said. "I really appreciate it, and I do enjoy it here. It's really just a matter of money. And like I said, it will be my secondary job."

He smiled again. "Right," he said. "I completely understand. You gotta do what you gotta do. No worries."

He turned and took a few steps away before stopping and turning back to me. "Just curious, how much would you need to make for this to be your only job?"

I scrunched my mouth to one side as I multiplied some numbers in my head. I thought about the loans I was currently paying, the other loans that would kick in three months from then, and of course, my rent. Finally, I said a number.

"Okay then, good luck at that interview" he said quickly as he turned around and walked away.

With that, I was set to attend a job interview for a valet position at a hotel. Thanks to the numerous jobs I had worked over the years, I had become pretty good at job interviews. I always believed that if you could put me in front of someone for an interview, I could get the job. It's getting in front of the person that's tricky.

But the hard part was over. It was time to nail this interview and start a second job.

Nailing the Interview

There's a lot of job interview advice out there. There are even books written about the subject. I can't imagine what they're filled with. Succeeding at a job interview is pretty simple:

- Don't be late
- Seriously, don't ever be late.
- Don't dress like a slob
- Act excited and friendly
- Do your best to make an impression (be memorable)
- Make eye contact
- When they ask you if you have questions, make sure you have questions
- Control the momentum of the interview

A great interviewee practically runs the interview. They smile, nod, and joke. They ask questions back to the interviewer. They convey the passion they carry for the potential job. If you can do all of those things, you've got a great chance of landing the job.

I'd probably hire you.

I'd also recommend coming up with a go-to question or statement to use in interviews. Something that will bring you up to the next level in the eyes of employers. A finishing move of sorts.

After all, competition for open jobs can be fierce. The person interviewing you has probably interviewed countless people with the exact same résumé and experience as you. How are you going to stand out? What's going to set you apart and let them know that **you** are the person they want for the job? The person they *need* for the job.

Hi, My Name is Timothy, and I Want to Park Cars

As it happened, my interview to become a valet was a group interview. I had never done a group interview before. But like all fierce predators, I adapted quickly. A lot of the same rules apply. The main difference is you're competing to be heard. Questions are asked not to individuals, but to the group as a whole.

I tried to answer second or third in the group. Speaking first made me seem overly eager, like I was more concerned with making sure I said something than I was with what I was actually saying.

In total, there were 12 of us being interviewed by three managers. At the end, one of the managers said that one of us interviewees was an undercover manager. They asked us to vote for who they thought the manager was. The group voted that I was the undercover manager.

I wasn't. I just made that strong of an impression. Like I said, I know how to do job interviews.

Out of the twelve, ten of us ended up being hired. The two that weren't consisted of a guy who was 10 minutes late to the interview and a guy who said about five words during the Q & A session. This reiterates the two most important parts of job interviews: be on time and make sure you talk.

After nailing the interview, all that was left between me and a second job was passing a urine test. Considering I had never done drugs in my life, I had nothing to fear (outside of a little stage fright). The test was a pretty mundane affair. You'd think that people working at a urine test facility would have a sense of humor about the whole thing. They don't. They're quite stoic. Like monks.

Monks holding cups of warm urine.

Regardless, I passed the test and was officially hired. I now was a college graduate with two jobs, neither of which required any amount of college education. But at least I was getting paid. In fact, for the first time in a very long time, my financial situation was surprisingly stable.

That was mostly because I was working all the time.

It didn't take long for the available hours at my valet job to rapidly increase. Turns out valet workers aren't always the most reliable employees. After working at my hotel for 2 months, the staff had almost entirely switched over. That put me in the upper echelon of both of my jobs. The money at valet was really good, so I didn't want to turn down any opportunities.

At the same time, I felt committed to Panera so I tried not to decrease hours there. This left me working anywhere from 60-70 hours a week. I probably pushed 80 a few times. That might sound terrible. Okay, at times, it was. But there are some distinct advantages to working all the time.

The Advantages of Working All the Time

I should preface this by saying there are those who *have to* work all the time and those that *choose* to work all the time. For those who have to work double shifts just to survive, I empathize with you. Stay strong, and try to plan a way out.

Now, if you're someone who's considering working all the time out of your own freewill, there are some perks. First, you'll be making more money than you need. Having a surplus of money is very nice at times. Pretty much all the time, actually. In addition to making more money than you need, you're also too busy to really do anything, so you don't spend a lot of money either.

It's amazing how much of your money gets eaten up by grabbing food with friends or heading out for the night or shopping so you have clothes for when you go out at night. If you're working all the time, you don't really need new clothes because you hardly wear the ones you have.

And since your money isn't being eaten up by small, regular expenditures, you can afford some bigger items. In the span of three months, I bought a brand-new TV, upgraded my entire desktop computer, and bought my first smartphone. And I still had extra money on hand. That Christmas, I bought all of my family members two presents.

Maybe I wasn't being as financially responsible as I could have been, but after being broke for so long, it was nice.

Also, because I was so busy working, I didn't have time to sit and dwell on my problems. I wasn't stuck in my apartment pondering what I was doing with my life. Instead, I kept busy with work. When I did have free time, I truly appreciated that free time. Hanging out with friends on weekends became a very big deal because I usually worked weekends.

However, as great as it is to have money and appreciate the time you have with friends, working all the time starts to wear on you.

The Disadvantages of Working All the Time

As I shifted my car into park, I leaned back against the headrest and stared at the tree branches through my sunroof. Closing my eyes, I breathed in heavily and held the air. The sun shined through my windows, warming my skin as I relaxed for a moment. I had no desire to move.

"What am I doing with my life?" I said, opening my eyes and running a hand through my matted hat-hair.

I had just pulled into my apartment parking lot after getting back from a 6am to 2pm shift at Panera. Now I had less than 15 minutes to go up to my apartment, change clothes, come back, and head off to work at my valet job. That would go till 11-11:30pm, after which I would come home, get to bed around midnight-12:30am, and wake up at 5am so I could go in at Panera again.

Days like this had become routine. Days where I worked 16+ hours. Days where I only went home to change or to sleep. Sometimes, I wasn't even able to go home between jobs, leaving me forced to change in bathroom stalls.

This was my life, and in the moments where everything cleared long enough for me to think, I wasn't sure if there was a point to it all.

This is the downside to working all the time.

Generally, you grow numb to the passing of time and to the struggles of your life. But in those rare moments where you catch a reflection of the life you're living, it's not pretty. You may feel trapped, suffocating under the constant schedule of work.

I had grown irritable. I often had zero patience with the people around me at Panera. I was also getting sick about once or twice a month. Since my sleep schedule was a mess, and I was going non-stop, my body wasn't particularly happy with me.

Why didn't I just quit? That seems like the obvious option here. But I was out of the poor-house, and I was very hesitant to return. Plus, all the work took my mind off the fact that I was a college graduate working as a valet and "catering coordinator". I had been promoted at Panera, but the truth is, the new title made my job much more miserable.

Meanwhile, at valet, the money was good, but the work was getting frustrating. My coworkers weren't always the most dependable people, my manager would schedule me when I wasn't supposed to be working, shifts were wildly unpredictable, customers were often condescending, and of course, there's the fact that hotels never close. Ever. Our front doors had no locks on them.

They didn't even latch.

In exchange for having Thanksgiving off that year, I worked Christmas. Eve *and* Day. More specifically, I worked till 11:45am on Christmas Eve and 7:00am on Christmas Day. I slept in my car in between. The heating of the parking garage was turned off that night, so it got a little cold. When I awoke the next morning, there were no presents for me. No stockings to be opened. Just cold, stale air and a runny nose.

Merry Christmas....

Finally, I couldn't take it anymore. Upon purchasing a lovely new TV for myself (after working nearly 40 hours in the span of 48 hours on New Year's Eve/Day), I decided it was time for a change. Initially, I reduced my hours at Panera, but once I got a little taste of freedom, I wanted the whole thing. Though hesitant to go down to one job, I realized that Panera was often holding me back from certain shifts at valet or occasionally forcing me to leave early when I could stay late and make more money.

So I typed out a magnificent two-week notice and handed it in.

My manager and coworkers were sad to see me go, and I was a little sad myself, but I was confident it was a good decision. Once again, life looked promising. I felt I had reached a turning point where, while I would still be a college graduate working valet, I would have time to write, to be with friends, and to live my life.

That feeling of hope didn't last long.

When It Rains, It Pours

At this point, it had been 10 months since I had graduated from college, and things certainly hadn't been easy. Between moving, working, and sorting out my post-college life, I had been pushed to my limits. But somehow, I kept it together. As I transitioned to one job, I found myself with considerable more time and thus, awareness to the world around me.

I realized I had lost a number of friendships since graduating from college. This is a harsh truth of college. Many of your closest friends will leave you or you will leave them, and you may be friends no more. Even with people who still lived in the area, I found myself disconnected from them, including one of my very best friends.

I was determined to fix this issue along with a number of other issues. I would repair my friendships, I would find a new, more fulfilling job, and I would start writing more. I was going to be someone!

Unfortunately, these dreams were built with straw, and in the span of a few short days, everything fell apart. I'm not going to go into detail, but some unfortunate events happened in my personal life that broke me and left me feeling incredibly alone.

That's when I hit rock bottom.

I could make it through the financial hardships, the insecurity, the lack of direction, and the loss of pride. But this last thing turned out to be one thing too many, and when that happened, my defenses shattered, leaving me open to a crushing wave of reality.

I was an exposed nerve.

In that moment, I saw my life through the most critical lens possible, and I realized I was working a mediocre job, living in an empty apartment with nothing to show for my 24 years of life. I was a joke, or at least I thought so, and that plagued me unceasingly every day.

I had trouble sleeping. I could barely eat. I lost 15 pounds that I didn't really have to lose. Every night, I had unpleasant dreams. Every day, my brain was racked with the hypotheticals of what I could have done differently with my life. It didn't help that I had a job that mostly consisted of me standing by myself, left alone with my own treacherous thoughts.

Then I had a panic attack. It was very confusing at the time. I had never had one before. There I was, sitting on my couch, watching *Harry Potter and the Half Blood Prince* when my chest tensed up and my heart started punching against my ribs, trying to rip its way through my body. I fought for each breath, forcing air into deflated lungs as I laid down and curled into the fetal position.

I always thought when people said it felt like the walls were closing in, they were being poetic, but it actually felt as though the walls were curving around me. I was helpless, trapped in my own paralyzed body as I waited for this calamitous moment to pass. It eventually subsided, and I immediately sprinted out of my apartment to get some fresh air and track down a friend or two.

But the emptiness was still there inside.

Finally, a few days later, I broke down and started crying. I should let you know that I am not a crier. A lot of people say that, but I mean it. To this day, I've never cried during a movie, wedding, funeral, song, etc. At that point in my life, I hadn't cried in 12 or more years. I kind of forgot what it was like. I would end up crying one more time, but thankfully, there were no further panic attacks.

Guard Your Heart and Stuff

Now, you may be wondering why I share this horrible time in my life. I share it because there's a good chance it could happen to you after college graduation (or whenever you decide to begin your adult life). I think I had this idea that all my personal and emotional drama played itself out in middle school, high school, and college.

I thought that when you reached your adult life, your problems were more on the financial and occupational side, save for the death of a loved one or getting a terminal illness. This time period served as a very strong reminder that my emotions were vulnerable regardless of how old I was. If anything, the emotional pains were much more real in my post-college life because they simply poured salt onto cuts left by my personal and professional failures.

People will talk in great length about getting a job after college or seeing the world or getting married or any number of big, cool, important things like that. What they don't really mention is the fact that you're still you, and thus, you're open to all the same doubts, fears, and heartbreaks that you've carried with you up to that point.

It's not as if the only problems you face are fancy, adult problems. All of those tiny, petty, and sometimes juvenile things that have torn at you since your teenage years will still tear at you. Your insecurities will remain your insecurities, and it is up to you whether you face them and overcome them, or let yourself be destroyed by them.

Mine got the best of me, and it took almost a year to put myself back together. The bad news is that year was the worst year of my life. The good news is it was followed by my life's turning point.

Keep Moving Forward

When you've been beaten down and your dreams have been trampled on, it's easy to become cynical. During my second year out of college, all I could do was work as a valet, sending out job application upon job application, hoping that someone out in the professional world would realize how awesome and talented I was.

I was putting out multiple applications every week. Sometimes I would receive a rejection email a few hours later. Other times I wouldn't receive a rejection at all. That was the worst. Apparently I wasn't even worth responding to, and through all of this, I began to think more and more that maybe I was neither awesome nor talented. I didn't understand what exactly I did wrong. I went to college. I got a degree. I rocked all of my writing classes. My professors told me I was a skilled writer. Wasn't I to be rewarded with a job now? What was I missing?

I didn't know, and no one was telling me. So I did the only thing I could do.

I kept at it.

Not only that, but I expanded my options and tried to leave a future "if-all-else-fails" option open. Those were two things I didn't really do while I was in college. And they say people don't learn from their mistakes.

To increase my chances of finding an opportunity, I started to look for jobs in other geographical locations. I wasn't going to move home, but there wasn't much to hold me to my current area either. So I applied to jobs near my siblings' homes. If I got a job in either of those areas, I could move in with them for a while until I got on my feet.

I also started asking more people how they got their jobs. There was my friend Tyler (a different Tyler than the one from before) who was making very good money on a two-year technical degree. He said I could be doing what he was doing with just a semester or two of college, and he could help get me a job. A coworker suggested looking into work as a paralegal. I investigated both options. Why not?

Meanwhile, since I was making good money at the valet job, I was eager to see if I could move up. After receiving an initial promotion, I was asked out to coffee with our district manager. He informed me that he had noticed my work ethic and invited me to join a manager training program they were starting. Completing that would open up the path to a lot of opportunities within the valet company.

Now, did I want to work at a valet company for the rest of my life? No. But that's where I was at the moment, and I was determined to make the most of it. To make it work for me. So I started manager training.

I didn't know exactly where I was heading at this point in my life, but I knew one thing. My days as an entry level valet worker were numbered. And wherever I ended up after that was going to be better. I was going to make certain of that.

Doing What You Can with What You Have and Where You're At

There will probably come a time in your life when you're not exactly where you want to be. I mean, not at all. Not even close to it. Whether it's with your job or where you live or your relationship status, or all of the above, you'll be standing there, looking up at the clouds, arms spread wide, screaming "Really?".

But just because you're not where you *want* to be doesn't mean you're not where you're *supposed* to be.

Sometimes you're supposed to be uncomfortable. Sometimes life needs to be difficult. This is what pushes people to do bigger and better things. The truth is, continuous comfort is overrated.

When you're at those places in life where you're stuck, that's the best time to prepare yourself for the next step. To work on the things you love. To remember your dreams and start chasing them.

Once the mad dash of two jobs was over, I hit a point where I felt stuck. Technically speaking, I was comfortable. The time of day I worked wasn't always the best, but switching shifts and getting time off was usually easy. I made good money. I had plenty of time to hang out with friends. I had joined a gym and started working out. I was driving this awesome Cadillac I was able to buy after totaling my previous car (it's a long story).

But I wasn't really doing anything with my life.

Sure, I was trying to get a new job. I was applying left and right. And I was also working my way up the valet ladder. At the end of the day though, I only had so much control over whether or not I would find a new job. As for the promotion, it was up in the air when that would happen. Even if I got it, it wasn't what I wanted to do with my life. It wasn't the reason why I sunk tens of thousands of dollars into collage.

One day, I was at home when I remembered an idea I had shortly after graduation. I had been sitting in my college apartment, processing the long list of mistakes I had made the previous 5 years, and I thought to myself *I could write a book on what **not** to do when you go to college.*

It was just a funny little idea that soon faded in the scramble for a job. Now, as I reflected on my first year and a half out of college, I realized just how much I had learned since that anticlimactic graduation. I knew all of these things I wished I had known before college. And I knew I wasn't the only one who had made a lot of mistakes during my collegiate career.

So I sat down and mapped out an outline for a book. A guide of "what not to do" if you're going to college. Two weeks later, I had finished the first draft of what would become this book. It was short, sloppy, and it didn't really have an end, but I had written something. Something that I was proud of and thought was important-ish.

And in that moment, I felt just a little bit better about life.

I also started a blog around this time. It was called *This Blank Page*, and it dealt with a lot of the thoughts and feelings I had been having in recent months. It's following was small, but I received some heartwarming feedback during that time. Even though I was still just a valet with a college degree, for the first time in a long time, I felt like I was finding an actual place in the world.

I felt like I was getting closer to doing whatever I was supposed to be doing. And in that moment, it was just enough to keep me sane. It helped me hold out just long enough to reach the shores of a new era.

It's Going to Be Worth It

"Needless to say," I said, "The past few months have been...interesting."

I looked up from my coffee to Steve who was sitting across from me.

"What now?" he asked.

"Not sure. I think I've basically tapped out my current markets."

"Maybe you need to move into a new market?"

"Maybe," I said before sipping up the last of my coffee. "Or maybe I need to improve my, uh, *résumé.*"

"What's wrong with your résumé?"

"Could be stronger. I think I'm still figuring a few things out, making sure I'm worthy and ready."

"Are you sure you're not just dragging your feet?"

"I've asked myself the same thing. But let's say an opportunity came along right now, I'm not sure if I'd even be ready to take it. I've waited this long. I don't really want to mess it up. And based off what's happened this past year, maybe some time off isn't so bad."

Steve sat silent for a moment, tapping his fingers against the side of his cup. "Hey, if you don't think you're ready, there's nothing wrong with that. Want to head out?"

"Yeah," I said before standing up.

As we walked out the door of the Barnes & Noble, I realized we had just been talking about my love life (or lack thereof) for nearly two hours. If you had walked by our table, you might have thought we were talking business, but the truth was, we were talking about women. If anything, I was specifically avoiding talking about business.

Ever since I had stopped doing work for him, communication between Steve and I had become essentially non-existent. He was busy with family things and running a business. I was busy trying to figure out what I was doing with my life and not crying anymore.

Also, there was the fact that I had based my entire post-college plans on the idea that I would be working for him upon graduating. Instead, work for Steve's business became less and less until it disappeared altogether. Was it Steve's fault? No. That didn't make it a whole lot less awkward. We had never really talked about it, and at this point, it seemed unnecessary to bring it up.

So we talked about my romantically challenged life. I guess that was fine. Steve had asked me a few days earlier if I had wanted to grab some coffee and catch up. "Sure," I said. A part of me had wondered if he wanted to talk business, but it appeared he didn't.

We got into his car and he drove me back to the auto shop where my car was having its oil changed. As I reached for the door handle, Steve stopped me.

"Hey," he said awkwardly," You don't have to answer this right now. In fact, don't. I want you to think about it."

"Okay..." I said confused.

"I was wondering if you would have any interest working part time writing and taking some pictures."

"You want me to write and take pictures?" I asked, trying not to smile.

"That's the idea."

"And you're going to pay me."

"Part time, yes."

"But you don't want me to respond right now?"

"I want you to make sure you want to do it because you want to do it. Not because you want money."

"Steve," I said, "If I wanted more money, I would get a second job again. You want me to write for a job. That's what I went for college for."

"Right. Okay."

And just like that, I had a part time job working for Steve's business. For $500 a month, I would write a few blog posts and every Tuesday, I would drive out to one of his clients' locations and take pictures of their new inventory. Nothing fancy, but it was certainly closer to what I wanted to do than valet was. So I said yes.

Eager to avoid the working trap I had fallen into before, I reduced my valet hours to four days a week. When I went home for Christmas that year, I was able to tell people that I was working for a web design and marketing company part time. It sounded a lot better than explaining that I was a valet in search of his life's purpose.

It was amazing how much of an impact a part time job had on my outlook. Sometimes, it's the little things that give you enough hope to hold onto. A glimmer of light leaves you believing that there just might be something better out there. Now that I was doing some work that left me feeling good though, I wanted more.

I knew I had to get everything out of this job that I could. Steve soon mentioned that he was planning to hire a full-time person in the near future. He couldn't promise when it would happen, or that I would be the one hired for it, but he hoped things would work out in my favor.

All I knew was I was going to do everything in my power to make sure that job came my way. I didn't stop applying elsewhere. I didn't stop my management courses at valet. But however I could, I worked towards getting this job for Steve's business. The job I had planned on having two years earlier.

Any project Steve threw my way, I'd tackle it. Every time he asked me to try and figure out how to do something, I figured out how to do it. I was hustling like this job was my only hope. At this point, it *was* my only hope.

"If I don't get this job," I had said to another friend of mine, "I have no idea what I'm going to do."

"Then get the job," my friend said.

If it's Meant to Happen, Make it Happen

"If it's meant to happen, it will happen."

Ever been told that before? Maybe you yourself have said that to someone. I don't buy it in most cases. I think that phrase is used so people feel better about missed opportunities. They figure that if something didn't happen that they wanted to happen, it wasn't their fault.

It wasn't meant to be, they will say.

But maybe it was meant to be, and they simply didn't act. Let's say you're meant to end up in a relationship with someone. If you never ask that person out, and they never ask you out, you probably won't end up in a relationship with them. It doesn't matter if the two of you were meant to be.

Maybe you don't believe that anything is meant to be, and things just happen. All the more reason to go out and make things happen then, right?

Personally, I believe that certain things are *meant to be*. But we are entirely capable of ruining those moments by making the wrong choices or choosing not to do anything at all. When you have opportunities placed before you, whether by chance or destiny, it's up to you to choose to go after them.

You may not have full control over the situation, but you have some. Only once you've done everything in your power can you say whether or not something was meant to be.

When I started working for Steve part time, I realized I had an opportunity at a career. I believed that I was meant to work at this job. After all, I had bet my future on this job when I graduated from college. And now, here it was.

It would have been easy to assume I was going to get it. I could have just sat back, did the minimum amount of work and left the rest up to chance. But I had come too far to do that. I was going to do everything I could to make sure I got the job.

Standing Spotlight

In the two years that followed my college graduation, I had hoped and waited for a proper job interview. One that was for a company I wanted to be at, where my experience and résumé would mean something. I had always said that if I could just get an interview, I could convince anyone that I was the right person for the job.

Trouble was, I never reached the interview stage. Time and again, I would apply only to be cut in the first round. I definitely wasn't the only one this happened to. I had one friend who applied to over 70 jobs in one month. In return, she received one call back (which didn't turn into a job).

But for me, that was about to change. Finally, I was going to get my interview. Finally, I was going to get my chance to shine. And I was ready.

A lot of people wait for their opportunity in the spotlight, that moment when they get to show the world what they're made of. Yet so few of them are actually ready for it. If someone actually came, sat down in front of them, and said "show me what you got", they would have little to nothing. I'm guilty of this. For years, I've wanted to be a writer, yet if some big publishing company actually wanted to read my stuff, I wouldn't have had anything worthwhile to show them.

You should always be ready, just in case.

Anyone who knows me knows that I have a habit of always having my hair done. I like to look presentable, no matter where I go. Why? Because I want to be prepared. I'm a guy who is single, and you never know who you might run into while out in the world. So I make sure to put my best foot forward.

I make sure I'm ready.

Granted, that hasn't really worked for me so far, but that's not the point. If you're looking to launch a career, you should set yourself up so that when that spotlight finally shines upon you, you've got something to show. This doesn't just include what you're doing professionally, but in some cases, what you're doing privately as well. Employers look at people's social media. If you're posting pictures of you getting hammered every other day, and you're saying derogatory things every other tweet, you could very well be damaging your chances of being hired.

Is that fair? It doesn't matter. That's how it is. Make yourself presentable.

All Part of the Plan

The job was officially posted for the world to see. By that, I mean it was listed on Craigslist. I had competition, and they were applying fast. Was I worried? Of course. There was a good chance that I was going against people who had better experience than I did. That was my biggest fear.

But Steve was kind enough to give me whatever advantages he could.

One of my part time duties was taking pictures of this car dealership's new inventory every Tuesday. On this particular Tuesday, Steve said he wanted to meet up with me afterwards for lunch. He was going to explain the kind of questions he would be asking in the interview.

Since this was the first full-time employee he was hiring, it was very important that they met all of his requirements. Most of our conversation consisted of him testing me on whether or not I really wanted this job. He expressed his concerns. He told me that if I didn't want to pursue this job, I didn't have to, and there would be no hard feelings. He also made it clear that I was in no way guaranteed this job, and when I walked in for the interview, it would be as if I didn't know him at all.

In response to all of this, I simply told him the truth: I wanted this job, and I was going to do whatever it took.

He nodded and said "Okay then, I guess you're ready."

We set a time for the interview, and then we walked outside towards our respective cars. I said goodbye and pulled my keys out of my pocket. Just as I was opening the door to my black Cadillac Seville, Steve stopped me.

"Well," he said, "you've got the job."

The keys fell out of my hand. "What?"

"If you want it," he said, "the job is yours."

"Huh?" I questioned again. My thoughts raced over the conversation we just had. The questions. The testing. The concerns. And that's when I realized I had been played.

Our lunch session wasn't a pre-interview meeting. It was the interview.

"You're serious?"

"Why don't you come over here, and we'll talk about it."

I scooped up my keys, walked over to where he was parked, and got in the passenger's seat. From there, we talked for another half an hour about my new job.

"You start in two weeks," he said. It wasn't a question.

"I'll start right now," I quickly said.

Steve smiled. "Two weeks. You'll need the time to prepare. We're throwing you straight in the fire."

If he was trying to scare me, it wasn't working. I was way too excited to be scared. And I was still a little bit in shock. Generally, I hate it when people say stuff like *good things happen when you least expect them to*, but that literally just happened to me. Steve continued to talk, but the details didn't really matter to me.

All that mattered is that I had done it. I had gotten the job. Two years of dead ends and broken dreams, and I had made it through to this moment.

I was actually beginning the next step of my life.

Grandma was Wrong

The hours that followed Steve's offer were a blur. I just remember this sudden weight being lifted off me. I called my parents to let them know their son wasn't a failure anymore. I'm pretty sure they responded with something like "Now all you have to do is find a wife", but even that didn't bother me. I had a job.

A job where I wouldn't be working weekends. I wouldn't have to work a holiday ever again. When I realized that, I almost started crying. Seriously, I was driving in my car, and the revelation of open holidays year-round made my eyes just a tad misty.

And in that moment, I thought back to something my grandma used to say:

"Honey, I have arrived."

See, my grandma didn't grow up with a lot. As she grew older and got married, her quality of life improved. That's not to say she lived in high society, but she felt as though she did. When she would walk into a fancy place or get on a big airplane, she would exclaim in her southern accent "Honey, I have arrived!"

And that's how I felt when I got this job. Like this was it. I had fought my fight, won, and now I got to sit on this big magical throne and rule over my subjects. It's easy to feel that way during life's victories. You might feel that way after you score a winning touchdown or graduate from high school or get that really cute person's phone number.

But these moments are never the end. More often than not, they're only the beginning. And that magical feeling is temporary. My grandma would exclaim that she had arrived when she boarded a nice plane, but once that flight was over, she still had a life to live. The same was true for me.

It's true for all of us.

Life goes on. We don't *arrive* as much as we just take another step forward, and then we keep going. You should recognize these moments.

Remember them. Celebrate them. They're beautiful moments worth remembering. But don't stop. Don't settle for that moment. That's how people let promising careers turn into jobs they hate. It's how they let the love disappear from their marriages. It's how they let their health go out the window.

Because they think they've arrived.

Victory is great, but what you do next might be the most important decision of your life. Remember that.

Side Note: The Victory Beard

As I said, it's good to celebrate your accomplishments. What's really great is to plan these celebrations in advanced. They can serve as extra motivation or simply something to look forward to. For example, I had a teacher in middle school who was a diabetic, so sugar was a no-go for him. But he told us he had a can of Coke in his office, and on his last day of work, he was going to drink that Coke no matter what.

I'm not sure that's the safest example to give, so here's what I did.

Before I got my job in the marketing and design world, I was a valet for almost two years. As a valet, I had to shave every time I worked. Every single time. If I had more than 24 hours' worth of facial hair on my face, my boss would say something to me. He'd even send guys to the bathroom with a razor from the front desk.

True story.

Having a very even spread of facial hair, I had been a 5 o'clock shadow guy for most of college. Walking around with a clean shaved face for two years was not enjoyable.

So I had told myself when I was done with the valet life, and I had myself a real job, I would grow a full beard. A *victory* beard as it were. I had never grown a beard before, and that seemed like as good a reason as any to do so.

Well, with a career path locked in, the stage was set for me to become a grizzly man. And I did. For a little over five weeks, I developed a fully-fledged beard. I even documented it across my social media (#victorybeard).

Then I shaved it off, and continued with my life.

Chapter 8:

Don't Lose Your Plot

As I was leaving my job at the hotel to begin a real career, I started doing what most people do when they leave a place. I thought back on the memories I had made there. Were my life a sitcom, this would have been an episode known as a "clip show", where the majority of footage consists of clips from previous episodes. I always liked those. I'm a sucker for nostalgia.

With valet, I hadn't even been there two years, and yet, there was no shortage of happenings. A lot of strange things go on when you work at a hotel late at night in the middle of a city. Many of those stories are things I will not repeat here. But there was one exchange that has always stayed with me.

On a particularly slow night, I was sitting at the front desk, talking to a friend behind the counter. I could tell she was kind of down, so I asked her if everything was alright.

"It just all feels kind of pointless," she said.

"Meyer's Briggs tests?" I asked.

"Life."

"Ah, that makes more sense," I said. "How long has it felt that way?"

"Since I graduated from college, I guess. I work two part-time jobs, and I don't care about either of them, and I go home at night, and I wonder what I'm doing with my life."

"That sounds familiar..." I replied.

"I just feel...numb. Directionless."

"Well," I said, "What are you doing?"

"That's the thing. I don't know. Have you even been listening?"

"I mean outside of work. Outside of these jobs. Are you involved in any groups or activities you care about?"

She paused for a moment. "No."

"Are you pursuing any life goals or future opportunities?"

"Not really."

"Is there anything you're doing with your life right now that you actually care about?"

There was a long pause. It wasn't that she was pondering her answer. She knew what she was going to say. She just didn't want to say it.

"No."

And there lay her problem. Once upon a time, she had a dream that had carried her from childhood to adulthood. It motivated her to enter college. It gave her strength to face each day. Her life was a story, and the next scene of that story was supposed to involve starting a great career that she was passionate about. But the picture became blurry and vague as she got caught up in all the little details that clutter up adult life.

The story grew stagnant until my friend had lost the plot of it altogether.

The Best Intentions. The Worst of Consequences

I love *The Last Samurai*. It's in my top 5 movies, no question. If I was the type of person who cried during movies (which I'm not), I would have cried at the end of this one both times I saw it in theatres. The whole movie is set around Japan trying to modernize its ways at the end of the 1800s. The Japanese emperor wants his people to be strong and unified. He wants his country to have all of the things the rest of the world has access to, and so, he begins to bring people from all over the world to modernize his country. While his intentions are noble, he ends up starting a civil war that results in the deaths of hundreds, including the Emperor's beloved teacher.

In one of the final scenes (*spoiler*), the Japanese emperor is presented with the sword of his former hero, the last true samurai. In that moment, he realizes what his actions had cost him. He realizes that though his intentions were pure and progress was made, he had lost his way. He had forgotten why he wanted to change his country.

When you try to move forward, it's easy to get caught up in the moment. When you get caught up in the moment, it's easy to forget who you are and what you value. I went to college for good reasons. I had big dreams for when I was done. Like my play from scriptwriting class, I had the story all worked out in my head.

But somewhere between the scramble of graduating and desperately looking for a job, I had forgotten what the point was. When you're focused on simply surviving, it's hard to focus on actually living. But if you're not truly living your life, what's the point of being alive?

Life will inevitably feel pointless when it's lived without purpose.

Like a story needs a plot, your life needs a purpose behind it to drive it forward. Hopefully you've caught some glimpse of that in your life already. You've looked into your grand storyline and where it might be heading.

Even still, if you go too long without reminding yourself why you're doing something, you'll forget that *why* altogether. I've seen it happen to friends. I've seen it happen to myself. I get distracted very easily, always wanting to start something new as soon as there's a dull moment in my current pursuit. It's probably a result of me being a habitual channel changer when I was younger. The second a commercial came up, I'd turn the station until another commercial came up. Next thing I knew, I was watching three shows at the same time.

But because my focus was so fractured, I really wasn't watching any show. I was just watching clips, catching fragments of a greater whole I couldn't understand because I wasn't staying focused.

The Most Important Thing You Might Ever Do

I've seen a lot of people's lives get shaken up shortly after big moments of victory. Whether it was after marriage or a big move or a new job or something else entirely. So much effort goes towards this big moment, and then it's over, and you're forced to return to normal life.

That's not always the easiest thing to do.

I experienced a little bit of this after high school graduation and then a lot of it after graduating from college. I put so much work into chasing this goal, and then I achieved it, and it was sort of like *now what?*

It's like in the movie *The Dark Knight* when the Joker says "I'm like a dog chasing cars. I wouldn't know what to do if I caught one."

We can all be that way sometimes. We forget the reason for the chase because we're so focused on the object before us. I said in the previous chapter that what you do after the victories in life can be even more important than the victory itself. Unlike movies and books, your life doesn't end when that big goal is achieved. It continues to a new chapter. As long as there's breath in your lungs, your life is a never-ending story. A good story always has a conflict. The main character wants something and something stands in the character's way of getting it.

What are you chasing after next? What's the bigger picture here?

When I finally got a real job, I promised myself that I wasn't going to settle. I wasn't going to pretend that I had reached the end and coast through life until I retired and died. I believed that greater things were still to come. So when I finished my very first day of work, I left the office, got into my car, drove to a coffee shop, got my computer out, and started writing.

But Timothy, a voice in my head said, *it's your first day. You worked hard for this. Relax and go home. Take a break. You can write later.*

It would have been so easy to just call it a day. To drive home, sit on the couch, fire up my PS3, and tune out for the rest of the evening. It will always be easy to make excuses. Excuses might be the easiest thing in the world to create. And that's why they are worthless. Because it takes nothing to make them, and they leave you with nothing in the end.

An excuse isn't a reason. More often than not, it's a lie told to cover up the reason.

That's why I went out and started writing that day. Because I had told enough excuses in my life, and they hadn't done a single thing for me.

Going Full Circle

When you manage to track down your first real job, it will probably be somewhat of an entry level position. An entry level position at a competitive company will probably pay better than, say a job at Wal-Mart, but it's probably not going to pay as much as you'd like it to.

This was the case with my first real job.

If I'm going to be honest, I actually started off making less money than I did as a valet. Why would I do such a thing? Because it's better to make less money doing something you enjoy than it is to make more money doing something that makes you miserable. Trust me. I've been on both sides. I am very glad I took a pay cut in exchange for a job that meant something to me.

That said, I had been broke before, and it was a place I never wanted to go back to. So what do you do when the path you want to follow doesn't provide enough to support you? You make sacrifices. In my case, I knew what I needed to do.

I needed to get a second job. Again.

Originally, I had considered staying on as a valet, but that would have involved me having to continue working weekends and having to shave. I didn't want to do either of those, so I went to the place that I knew would hire me in a second.

Panera-freaking-Bread.

This is why you don't burn bridges when you leave places. Instead, you leave them sad to see you go, so that if a day comes when you return, they will welcome you with open arms. Did I imagine I would *ever* return to Panera? No. But there I was, a college graduate with a fulltime job who was ready to put on a hat and an apron once more.

And you know what? It really wasn't that bad. Actually, it was kind of fun most of the time. It helped that I was choosing to be there. When I initially worked there, it was an act of desperation. This time, it was a meditated decision. I knew it was the right choice.

I spent almost a year working at Panera part time, waiting. Waiting for my main job to develop, for my finances to stabilize, and to make sure I was on the right track this time. In that year, I made new friends and new memories, but the most important thing that happened took place shortly before I left.

I was at Panera one day, talking to a coworker. Like many of the people I worked with, he was on the verge of graduating from high school.

"You know," I said, "when I originally started here, we had to cut all the meats and cheeses by hand. You guys have it easy now."

"Are you trying to sound old," Alex asked, "Or do you just naturally say these things?"

"I think it's a bit of both."

"You have been here a long time."

"Not really though. I have yet to work here an entire year. The first time, it was about 9 months. It's only been 9 so far this time."

"So it's quitting time again?"

"Actually, if I can let you in on a secret, it's close. Just waiting for a couple things to come through at the real job."

"Oh boy," Alex said sarcastically. "How's this place going to run without you?"

"But actually, how is it going to run when I leave AND when all of you guys graduate and leave?"

He laughed. "They're basically screwed."

"Pretty much. You ready to get out of here? Go to college? All that jazz?"

"I think so," he said. "Any wisdom to pass on?"

"You should..." I paused. "Actually, if I gave you something I wrote, would you read it?"

"Seriously?"

"Yeah," I said. "It was a project I started after I graduated from college. Kind of abandoned it. Maybe you could help me decide if it's worth finishing."

"Definitely!" he said "Is it about you?"

"Me. Some of my friends. A family member or two. It's basically about everything I wished I knew going into college."

"This sounds awesome!"

"I wouldn't get too excited. It's a bit rough around the edges. I'll send what I have."

So I sent him a very rough draft of this book. Actually, it was two or three versions of this book Frankenstein-ed together. He was the target audience I was writing to, so I decided his opinion would determine if I finished writing it or not. I sent it via Facebook, and then I waited.

A mere four hours later, he responded back.

Alex: Thank you for sending me this. It was awesome, a great read and was just so cool to hear about your experiences. This could be something special.

Me: Really? You sure you aren't saying that because you know me?

Alex: Seriously. This could be a legit book!

Me: I think that's exactly what I needed to hear. Thank you SO MUCH for taking time to read it.

(Then he said something rather unexpected)

Alex: Oh, one more thing.

Me: Yeah?

Alex: I hope it's okay. My parents are reading it now. I told them too.

Me: Whaaaa...OF COURSE! So you really did like it.

Alex: You write like an old sage that is all knowing and inspirational.

Me: You know I'm going to have to quote that in the book.

I talked to him a few days later to get some more details and to hear what his parents thought. They liked it as well. They felt it talked about things a lot of people don't talk about. Considering that was the whole point of writing it, it was probably the best thing a person could say about it.

Between Alex and his parents, I had exactly the motivation I needed to resume work on this book. It felt like I was supposed to finish it. A few weeks later, I left Panera, transitioning to working one job again. But this time, it was a job that mattered to me.

And I felt like I had come full circle.

When I first entered Panera, I was a mess. I had no idea where I was going or what I was doing. As I left this time, I knew exactly what I was doing, why I was doing it, and I felt good about my place in life for the first time in a long time. Things felt right, like they were supposed to be this way.

I couldn't help but admire this beautiful symmetry as it unfolded. Maybe this wasn't the way things were supposed to have happened. Maybe I was supposed to make wiser decisions and have better finances and been more proactive in a job search, but everything worked out in its own way.

Never Forget

It's important to remember the things that have happened in your life. You don't want to dwell in the past or get hung up on the glory days, but you shouldn't forget where you've been, what you've gone through, and why you did it. There are reasons why we keep track of history.

To remember. To learn. To reflect.

It should be the same for your own personal history. Sometimes, it's hard to know where you're going without remembering where you started. Sometimes you can't fully appreciate what you have now if you've forgotten what you lacked in the past.

Never forget your trials. Your dreams. The good and the bad. And most importantly, don't forget who you are. You will change, grow, and develop, but somewhere deep down inside is the person you've always been. The person you were meant to be. The main character at the heart of your life's story.

If you lose that character, you'll lose the plot. If you lose the plot, you'll lose your purpose.

Lose your purpose, and you've lost everything.

Final Chapter:

Do Good

In the final scene of the final episode of *Boy Meets World*, the main cast is gathered in the classroom where the show began years earlier. Standing in front of them is Mr. Feeney, the man who taught them since they were little kids. Before they head off to face the rest of their post-college life, they ask thei r favorite teacher for one last piece of advice. This is what he says:

"Believe in yourselves. Dream. Try. Do good."

To which the character Topanga responds, "Don't you mean 'do *well*'?"

And Mr. Feeney smiles and says, "No, I mean *do* good."

Part of the reason I like the moment so much is because it speaks to the grammar nerd in me. But beyond that, it is just simple, beautiful advice. For someone starting a new chapter of their life, it's about the best advice someone can give you.

Do good.

Don't just do things for money or for fame. Don't do them to impress people or so you can post that cool Insta'. Do it because it's the right thing to do. Because it's what you're supposed to do. Because it's good. I can't help but think if people focused a little less on doing *grand* things and a bit more on simply doing *good* things, the world could be a better place.

And the beauty of doing something good is it doesn't matter what place you're at in your life. Anyone can do good in their own way. It might be some small act of kindness. It might be volunteering once a week. It might be simply smiling when you order your morning coffee. You have the ability to do good. So do it. You'll be amazed at the effect it has not just on your life, but on the lives of everyone around you.

Goodness, kindness, acts of love. They're contagious.

The Best is Yet to Come

When I was in high school, people always used to tell me that I was living the best years of my life, and I hated that. It's not that I didn't like high school. I loved my time during high school. But I didn't want to believe that that's as good as it got. That the rest of life was this downhill slope into bitterness and disappointment.

Having been outside of high school for a while now, I understand what those people meant when they said it. And I completely disagree with it. Yes, there are moments in high school that you will never experience again. There are things you can do in high school, actions that you can get away with that you can't once you are older.

But as great as your late teens can be, you can be very limited. You might be bound to where your parents live. Your job eligibility is determined by your age. Your schedule is set by family and teachers and coaches and all of the other people in your life. Though you're still capable of doing a lot as a high school student, you most likely live in a world with very defined walls.

As you grow older, especially heading into college and then exiting college (or just skipping over college altogether), those walls because smaller and further apart until they are nearly non-existent. In a world without boundaries, there might be less to protect you, but there's also less to restrain you.

And that leads me to believe that the greatest things are still to come.

You may be in a place right now where you think your best years are behind you. I've been there too. After I graduated from college, I remember driving past schools and thinking about how good I used to have it. I wished I could go back to the days where there was less responsibility. Where I just went to school and hung out with my friends and played videogames.

There's no going back though. I had to press forward, and when I did, things got much better. The truth is, the past life I longed to return to probably wasn't anywhere near as great as I remembered it being anyway. Hindsight has a tendency to lie to you.

Greater things are coming. The best things. Believe it.

Please, Whatever You Do, Don't Panic

It amazes me that at the age of 23, I felt old. I felt stuck. I was adrift in the sea of life with no shore in site, and the further I drifted out, the more I began to believe that this was how the rest of my life would be. Over the course of a year, the feeling kept building as I continued to float on until finally, I broke. I panicked.

And it changed nothing.

You may reach a point where life is stacked against you. Please, don't panic. It won't do you any good. In fact, it will probably make things worse. Instead, keep your perspective adjusted. Perspective is a powerful thing. On my 21st birthday, I dislocated my toe. No, it did not involve alcohol. After being taken the emergency room, the doctor told me that he was going to numb the toe so we could snap it back into place.

In order to numb it, he had to shove a needle the size of a dagger into my toe three times. It hurt. A lot. I gripped the rails of the hospital bed and lifted my body into the air as he drove the sharp metal tip into my skin. In the moment, I thought *what is he doing!? Why is he hurting me!?*

But a minute later, he grabbed onto my toe, and with a quick jerk, he popped it back to where it should be. I didn't feel a thing. If I wasn't watching it, I probably wouldn't have even realized it happened. As much as the numbing injection hurt, it saved me from the pain of my toe being straightened. I'm no doctor, but I'm assuming that would have hurt a lot more. That's the power of perspective. In the moment, the injection was terrible, and I couldn't wait for it to be over. In the grand scheme of my visit though, it was completely worth it.

What seemed like an unfair punishment served as the catalyst for me to move forward.

Oscar Wilde once wrote "Behind every exquisite thing that existed, there was something tragic". That might be a little melodramatic, but you get the point. You can't have the spring without the winter. You can't give life without the labor pains.

What if instead of panicking, you simply pushed harder. For all you know, everything in your life could be on the edge of getting better. You could be mere moments from your breakthrough when all those obstacles become memories. In the span of seven months, I went from having no idea where my life was going to having a career that I always wanted.

I could have never known that I was that close, but I hoped that I was. I believed that it would come to pass. And finally, it did. Once I stopped panicking. Once I stopped focusing on all those things out of my control and simply pressed forward.

It's not too late for you. You're not past some point of no return, whether you're 16 or 46. Go to school. Go *back* to school. Apply to your dream job. Write that book you've been pushing off. Run a marathon. Record an album. Make plans. Dream dreams. The rest of your life is right in front of you, waiting to be seized.

I've heard it said that in mixed martial-arts, you can escape from any hold. You just have to find the right pivot point. I like to think it's the same with life.

Like You're Not Even the Same Person

Remember Ryan, the worst college student ever? He had dug himself into a seemingly inescapable hole. On top of that, he wasn't a particularly motivated person. It would be easy to assume that his story ended there, with him living out the rest of his days in his hometown, working a dead-end job, buried in debt, drinking away his sorrow.

Thankfully, that is not the case.

Shortly after his failed first year, Ryan took another try at college. This time, however, he went to a very small, Christian-based college located in a tiny little North Dakota town. It was an environment where it was significantly harder to get into trouble. Still, he struggled his first year there, finding himself on academic probation.

Things started to turn around shortly after he met a girl named Kimberly. Kimberly saw something in Ryan that many others didn't at the time: potential

Sure, he had his flaws. He struggled with focusing and motivating himself, and he wasn't a great test taker, but Kimberly realized he was also very smart and quick to learn new things. So she helped him study, she pushed him to focus, and she encouraged him to pursue better goals.

Long story short, Ryan turned his life around, and in the process, the two fell in love and got married. After Kimberly graduated, Ryan transferred schools and got his own degree. Not only did he finish college, but he graduated with honors. Soon after, he got a great job in his field.

Now, they have three kids, a house, and a dog. Oh, and I should also mention that Kimberly is my sister, which makes Ryan my brother-in-law. He is legitimately one of the hardest working guys I know. Hearing stories of his past, I have a hard time believing that it's him. That guy that he was, the college dropout who lost his license, it's a completely different person.

That's not to say you need to meet that special someone before you can get your life in order. Often, relationships can make things harder and/or more complex. What Ryan's story shows is the importance of simply having someone who believes in you, who sees the things hidden beneath the surface. Had Ryan never met my sister, it's very likely he would have flunked out of college. Again.

In my own life, if I didn't have people who encouraged me, who said my writing spoke to them, I would have never finished this book.

And just as important, Ryan's story shows that the worst of predicaments can be dramatically turned around. You can escape your past. You can begin again. You can reach a place where it's like you're not even the same person you used to be.

If it Makes You Happy...

"Do what makes you happy". You've heard that before, right? It's everywhere. You probably have a friend on Facebook right now whose cover photo features that quote. It's not necessarily bad advice, but it should come with an asterisk or something next to it. See, I've learned that there are a lot of things that can make you happy in the moment but leave you feeling empty in the long-run.

Really, they're just bad decisions masquerading as a good time.

On the flipside, there are a lot of things that will make you happy in the long-run that aren't fun in the moment. Looking at my own life, I think of a few of the things that make me genuinely happy: playing music, staying in shape, writing, spending time with friends that I care about. None of these things came easily.

Learning to play the guitar starts with literally torturing your fingertips until they're tough enough to hold down the strings. Lifting weights for the first time is mostly just an exercise in embarrassment. Hiding away in coffee shops night after night, writing this book was not always a ton of fun. And when I think about the first time I met most of my close friends, it was just a giant session of awkward. A true friendship takes work. It's not just a big party from the start.

But it will leave you with happiness. With joy.

All of these things do that for me. If I would have just gone for whatever made me happy at the time, well, I don't really even want to think of where I'd be. So instead of saying "do what makes you happy", maybe we should change it to "do what will make you happy".

Or "do what will bring you happiness in the long run"?

That's kind of a mouthful. We can discuss it later. I'm open to suggestions.

Going back to the idea of "doing good", it's not something that's always instantly gratifying. It's a long-term goal that rarely involves taking the easy path. But it'll leave you and others happy in the end. So do it.

A Message to My Teenage Self (aka, the Recap)

Well folks, we're almost to the end. But before we go our separate ways, I want you to join me as I travel back in time to the year 2004. A 17-year old Timothy Wayne Snyder has just walked into Sheldon High School to begin his senior year. It's early in the morning, and the school is mostly empty. He's wearing a black t-shirt that says "New York City" in big letters on the front. I approach my younger self, disguised in a hat, sunglass, and fake mustache.

"Timothy Snyder," I say.

"Ummm, yeah...?" past Timothy says, brows raised in surprise under his shaggy bangs.

"Come with me if you want to live," I say in my best Austrian accent.

"Huh?" Past-Tim is a little rusty on his Terminator references and clearly afraid he's about to be abducted.

"Sorry," I say, "I've always wanted to say that. Don't worry, I'm not going to hurt you. In fact, I'm here to help you. I...I want to tell something."

The younger me starts looking at the corners of the ceiling. I think he's checking for hidden cameras. "And what's that?"

"I want to tell you everything that nobody told me about life after school. But first, let's sit down somewhere."

Seventeen-year-old Timothy is still skeptical, yet there's a familiarity about me he can't quite shake. He nods, and we walk to an empty cafeteria, taking seats at a table. I remove my sunglasses and place them before me, looking into the eyes that were mine 10 years ago. They're wide with hope and worry and curiosity, and I can't believe just how much I've changed and aged. I think of all the memories I carry that he has yet to experience.

Finally, I take a deep breath and begin.

"A lot of people are talking about college right now. As much as you've heard already, you're only going to hear more this year. It's going to be everywhere, raining down upon you, and at times, you'll feel like you're drowning in the mystery of what you're going to do with your life.

"But before you leave this town behind and head out into the world, I want you to know that whatever you do next, wherever you go from here, it starts with a choice. Your choice. Whether you're going to college or launching into a new career or traveling halfway across the world, own the decision that you make. And know why you're doing it. Don't just buy into the hype and do whatever it is that everyone is expecting you do it.

"Don't go to college because you feel you have to. Do it because *you* know it's what *you're* supposed to do.

"But don't be stupid about it. Even if you're pursuing the right path, you can make a lot of wrong choices while doing so. Take some time, plan things out. As Shakespeare would say, go 'wisely and slow. They stumble, those who run fast.' I know you own Romeo + Juliet, and you've watched it far more times than you'd care to admit, so you've definitely heard that before. Remember it.

"And don't undervalue practicality. A little practicality can go a long way. This includes having a back-up plan. The future can be very unpredictable. Even if you go to college and graduate like you planned, it might not be everything you hoped and dreamed. You might not want to do the job you planned to do. An opportunity you thought was a sure thing might end up falling apart. You have to be ready for that.

"That doesn't mean you can't have fun on the way. Enjoy yourself. Make memories. Have a great time. Live your life.

"But know that it's not going to be all fun and games. There will be hardships. You will hit walls and have bad days. You're going to be pushed and challenged more than you ever have been. You're going to experience hurt and disappointment like you didn't know you could. But it's going to be worth it. Whatever you do, don't forget that. Don't forget why you started this journey in the first place, why you're here on this earth.

"You're here to do something. Something good. Not just for yourself, but for the world around you. A little goodness goes a long way."

The teenaged Timothy stares in awe. "But..." he says, "But what exactly am I supposed to do? What *is* my purpose?"

"I think you have some idea already. The rest, you'll figure out along the way."

He picks nervously at the reddish sideburns on his head. Why I thought those were a good idea for us to have, I'm still not sure.

"But how do you know?" he asks.

In one quick motion, I tear the mustache off with one hand and remove my hat with the other. "Because I'm you."

The younger me almost falls off his chair. Now he gets it, the familiarity that he felt. He knows it's true. "Thank God, I don't get fat again!" he exclaims.

"Not yet, anyway."

"I have so many questions."

"I'm sorry, but I have to be getting back." I stand up from the table.

"Wait!" he pleads, raising a hand up. "Just one question."

I sigh and look at my watch. "Okay, one question."

"Am I...are we...still single?"

"I, uh, gotta go." And with that, I fade back through time and space into the present where I'm sitting at a table in a coffee shop, typing up the end of a book I've taken far too long to finish writing.

And for a moment, I consider rewriting the entire thing as a pseudo-science fiction, time-travel story. The thought quickly passes as I realize it's not about changing my past; it's about using my past to hopefully change someone's future.

So I put my hands on the keys one last time and begin writing the final section....

Parting Words

Thanks for taking the time to read this. I hope the words I've shared here helped you, even if it's in the smallest of ways. I definitely don't have all the answers. If I did, I'd probably be rich. Trust me, I am not rich. Maybe you disagree with everything I've said. Great. Feel free to disregard all of my advice and blaze a new trail entirely. Nothing would make me happier than to see you succeed in ways I couldn't even dream of.

If you did happen to like this book, could I ask you a favor? Share it with someone. Not just any someone, but someone specific whom you think would benefit from the stories I've told. I didn't write this book for myself. It wasn't some form of therapy or ploy to become famous. I wrote it to help people make better choices and to encourage them to not lose hope.

Whatever you do, wherever you go from here, tell a good story with your life. I used to see life as a checklist. The problem was, when I missed something on the list, everything fell apart. Now I see life differently. I see it as a story. A grand, never-ending story that continues with each passing day.

Stories have ups and downs. They have slow parts and fast parts. They have conflict, and then, they have resolution. Stories are beautiful.

Everyone loves a good story. And that's how your life should be. It should be beautiful. You should love it.

Go. Do good. Live your life. Love your life.

The End

Like the Book?

Make sure to leave a review on Amazon.com.

Find additional stories, advice, and resources for college and

young adult living at:

www.THATCOLLEGEBOOK.com

Share Your Story

Send an email to **Timothy@thisblankpage.com** and share

your own story about life after high school. I'd love to hear it!

About the Author

What can be said about Timothy Snyder that you didn't just read in the book above this? It's basically his life story. You probably know more about him than you care to. But if, for some reason, you wish to know more, here you go....

Timothy is a writer based in the magical Twin Cities metro of Minnesota. With this book now finished, he hopes to complete one of the two other books he started writing in the past couple of years. Occasionally, he posts random musings on his blog, **ThisBlankPage.com**.

When he's not writing, Timothy enjoys playing the guitar and piano, staying current with movies, video games, and pop-culture, and going to concerts. For his real job, he works at a web design agency called Radiate. It's a pretty cool place. If you think Tim seems like an alright person, you can follow him on social media at these places:

Twitter: @thetimsnyder

Instagram: @thetimsnyder

Facebook: That College Book

Alright, Tim is done talking in the third person now. Stay safe out there!

Made in the USA
Columbia, SC
06 April 2019